LF

THE SHORT NARRATIVES OF E. M. FORSTER

The Short Narratives of E. M. Forster

Judith Scherer Herz

St. Martin's Press   New York

First published in the United States of America in 1988

Printed in Hong Kong

ISBN 0–312–00912–7

Library of Congress Cataloging-in-Publication Data
Herz, Judith Scherer.
The short narratives of E. M. Forster.
Bibliography: p.
Includes index.
1. Forster, E. M. (Edward Morgan), 1879–1970—
Criticism and interpretation.   I. Title.
PR6011.058Z684   1987   823'.912   87–14447
ISBN 0–312–00912–7

For my father, Philip Scherer
1898–1972

Contents

Acknowledgements

Parts of Chapters 3 and 4 first appeared in 'The Narrator as Hermes: A Study of Forster's Short Fiction', in G. K. Das and John Beer (eds), *E. M. Forster: A Human Celebration* (London: Macmillan, 1979; New York: New York University Press, 1979); 'The Double Nature of Forster's Fiction', *English Literature in Transition*, 21 (1978) pp. 254–65; 'From Myth to Scripture: An Approach to Forster's Later Short Fiction', *English Literature in Transition*, 24 (1981) pp. 206–12.

I wish to thank the Society of Authors as the Literary Representatives of the Estate of E. M. Forster, and the Provost and Scholars of King's College, Cambridge, for permission to use unpublished materials. I wish also to thank Mrs Valerie Eliot for her permission to quote from a letter of T. S. Eliot to E. M. Forster, and Dr Michael Halls, the Modern Archivist, King's College, for his courtesies, counsels, and deft and rapid assistance, which made working at the Library so great a pleasure.

My largest debt of gratitude ('still paying, still to owe') is to my friend and colleague Robert K. Martin. He encouraged the book's first undertaking and has read it in every stage of its development; his thoughtful questions and comments have been essential to the evolution of the argument. Claude Summers, too, has been a careful and encouraging reader from the start. My son, Nathaniel, offered cautionary words and a challenging reading, and my daughter, Rachel, interest and affection. To them, to my husband and my mother, and to my father if I could, my thanks.

J. S. H.

List of Abbreviations

Page references to the sources listed below appear, where convenient, in the text, identified by the abbreviations given below. Abbreviations relating to published works are omitted where there is repeated reference to the same text. In Chapter 6 references to Montaigne also appear in the text, as explained in note 2 to that chapter.

AE   Forster, *Albergo Empedocle and Other Writings*, ed. George Thomson (New York: Liveright, 1971)

AH   Forster, *Abinger Harvest* (London: Edward Arnold, 1936)

AS   Forster, *Arctic Summer and Other Fiction*, Abinger Edition (London: Edward Arnold, 1980)

CB   Forster, *Commonplace Book*, facsimile edition, ed. Philip Gardner (Stanford, Calif.: Stanford University Press, 1985)

CE   Virginia Woolf, *Collected Essays*, ed. Leonard Woolf (London: Chatto and Windus, 1966–7)

CT   Forster, *Collected Tales* (New York: Alfred A. Knopf, 1975)

LTC   Forster, *The Life to Come and Other Stories*, Abinger Edition (London: Edward Arnold, 1972)

PP   Forster, *Pharos and Pharillon* (London: Hogarth Press, 1923)

TC   Forster, *Two Cheers for Democracy*, Abinger Edition (London: Edward Arnold, 1972)

Fur   P. N. Furbank, *E. M. Forster: A Life*, 2 vols (London: Secker and Warburg, 1977, 1978)

L&F   Mary Lago and P. N. Furbank (eds), *Selected Letters of E. M. Forster*, 2 vols (Cambridge, Mass.: Harvard University Press, 1983, 1985)

KCC   Unpublished materials in the Forster archives, King's College, Cambridge

1

Introduction

Two definitions of the essay, worlds apart in their time, place and frame of reference, but both equally magisterial in their claims, provide suggestive markers for the boundaries of this study. The first is pronounced emphatically in the voice of Dr Johnson: the essay is 'a loose sally of the mind; an irregular, undigested piece'. The second is more slyly spoken by Roland Barthes some 220 years later: 'l'essai s'avoue *presque* un roman: et un roman sans noms propres'; it is a novel without proper names.[1] If one definition would deny narrative coherence to the essay, the other seems to claim it on a grand scale. But a novel without proper names is a novel in which the generating imagination does not fragment and then reconstitute itself through specified, i.e. named, others, characters about whom actions are contrived and stories told. Character in the essay is the speaking self, at once subject and object ('I am myself the substance of my book', in Montaigne's seminal phrasing). Action in the essay is the movement of mind on matter, loose sallies, that take the form, in Bacon's words, of the 'dispersed meditation'.[2]

As a way of characterizing Forster's writing, moreover, such definitions have an immediate resonance, especially as they can apply as readily to his short stories as to his essays. What Bacon calls 'meditation' is perhaps looser and more dispersed in the essay, more concentrated in the story, but that word describes both forms equally and points as well to what is their most important creation – that is, the voice that utters them. It is a voice that neither in essay nor in story pretends to any privileged knowledge or special authority. That voice is, in fact, a character whether properly named or not, and so intimate and singular is it that one is tempted to call it by *its* 'proper name'. Indeed the title of the text from which the Barthes definition comes, his late *almost* autobiography, *Roland Barthes par Roland Barthes*, is particularly apt here. For Forster's stories and essays, in so far as they are much closer to the sources of his imagination than are his novel's social gestures and graces could collectively be given such a title as well.[3]

Thus, in this study, story and essay will be regarded less as

1

distinct genres than as aspects of a single process – narrative. Nonetheless, a definition of narrative that holds both forms in its embrace may seem unnecessarily elastic and non-discriminating. It can be justified, I believe, not only by appeal to the markedly cross-generic writing of Forster and his Bloomsbury contemporaries, but also by a view of narrative constructed syncretically out of two sometimes opposed approaches to that subject. If one follows Barbara Hardy or Peter Brooks, for example, one can so define that familiar but now suddenly problematic and elusive noun, 'narrative', as to contain nearly all genres. That is, terms such as 'novel', 'story', 'tale', 'romance', 'fantasy', 'autobiography' are seen to refer to merely local and, in a sense, provisional arrangements of what is understood from such a point of view as a primal, indeed biologically determined, act. In Hardy's view, 'Narrative . . . is not to be regarded as an aesthetic invention . . . but as a primary act of mind transferred to art from life.' In Brooks's, 'We live immersed in narrative, recounting and reassessing the meaning of our past actions, anticipating the outcome of our future projects, situating ourselves at the intersection of several stories not yet completed.'[4]

Hardy's view of narrative is different from Brooks's more formalist position, which, while resisting generic absolutes, does not deny their organizing power. Brooks is closer to the Czech novelist Milan Kundera, whose reinvention of his form impels him back to its origins in Diderot and Sterne, as he defines the novel in terms that imply nearly all other genres:

> A novel is a long piece of synthetic prose based on play with invented characters. . . . By the term synthetic I have in mind the novelist's desire to grasp his subject from all sides and in the fullest possible completeness[:] Ironic essay, novelistic narrative, autobiographical fragment, historic fact, flight of fantasy.[5]

But Kundera blurs generic distinctions in order to privilege *a* genre – the novel. Furthermore, he works with assumptions that are quite different from those behind the positions of Hardy or Brooks; that are, indeed, closer to the formalist assumptions of Gérard Genette, for whom narrative is 'singular, artifical and problematic' and whose theory of narrative is constructed to refute the premise that 'nothing is more natural than to tell a story'.[6] For Kundera's use of such phrases as 'synthetic prose' or 'desire to grasp his subject' depend on a view of narrative as 'aesthetic invention' even if the means of that invention are not generically limited or constrained.

'Synthetic prose' seems to me to be a precise description of Forster's writing as well. It keeps the emphasis on the organizing, i.e. synthesizing, powers of the writer-artificer at the same time as it suggests the created, shaped artifact that results. The label one attaches to that result is obviously less important than a description of the process that shaped it. Indeed, if one were following Genette, one would have to use 'discourse' rather than 'narrative' for many of Forster's short texts, for these more often 'openly adopt a perspective that looks out on the world and reports it' rather than one that 'feigns to make the world speak itself and speak itself as story'.[7] But neither term holds firmly, just as the natural and the artificial need not provide mutually excluding categories. Thus, while, with Hardy and Brooks, I assume the naturalness, indeed the inevitability, of narrative, I also assume the artificiality of any text we read. Novel, epic, essay, tale and story are artifacts begotten by artifice whose means (conventions, forms, genres, modes) are not simply there in the air we breathe, but are more or less available in different ways at different times and impose constraints on the creative and interpretative freedom of both writer and reader. The particular shape these artifices and constraints took in Forster's writing, and the interpretative power they grant the contemporary reader will form the basis of this inquiry. This will involve isolating those elements common to both story and essay as these emerge from a set of literary traditions and conventions, from a nexus of experience and values, from a moment of history and from the cultural and personal assumptions encoded in a response to that 'history'.

The competing and often conflicting positions derived from recent critical practice are invoked here not from any partisan position but to provide as wide a range as possible of potentially illuminating approaches to Forster's work. This is not a theoretical study in the sense that it advances its own theory or even attempts to make its readings serve one particular theory – an admission made in full awareness of its implicit theoretical bias. I nonetheless use – eclectically and non-systematically – those findings of contemporary narrative theory that can with least violence be brought to bear on Forster's writing. However, a powerful constraint throughout this project, despite the language of these introductory pages, derives from my awareness of Forster's avowed anti-theoretical bias and a sense, too, that the critic's language should never silence her subject's, the more particularly when the matter at hand is voice, and a voice that requires, in fact creates, its own listening-space.

I begin by looking at those texts that most obviously straddle the boundary between essay and story, in an attempt to place them historically in terms of the development of the short story as that form emerged from the essay (or, more precisely, as it emerged from the tale through the mediation of the essay), as well as contextually in terms of Forster's *oeuvre*. After that initial discussion, I examine each genre separately, but with greater emphasis on the essay in so far as it was gradually made to absorb the deeply personal myth-making that characterized the early stories. This shift can be marked by the publication in 1923 of *Pharos and Pharillon*, by which time the essay had replaced the story as Forster's personal text. However, it was a personal text that over the next thirty-five years took a conspicuously public form in newspaper, periodical and broadcast. Thus one of the chief preoccupations of the latter half of this book is the attempt to locate the often-quoted statements from these essays and talks in terms of their immediate political and cultural contexts and their private sources of belief, as well as within the context of the more recent debate over the significance and implications of Forster's deeply committed liberal humanism.

In Chapters 6 and 7, I examine the ways in which Forster expressed his belief in the individual as the reference point of value and insisted on the connection between the ethical and the aesthetic. This discussion involves a close examination of his *Commonplace Book*, as it provides both source and illumination for his more widely known anti-fascist and civil-libertarian writing. The assumption that there can be no gap between ethics and aesthetics is fundamental as well to an assessment of his literary criticism, a discussion that I place, in part, in the context of his relationship with Virginia Woolf. It was a friendship that was sometimes tensed and competitive, occasionally baffled and misunderstood (often by the participants themselves), but it was essential, indeed sustaining, for each of them. Both the Forster–Woolf contention and the debate over Forster's statements about friendship, loyalty and the state have frequently been enlisted in partisan attacks and counter-attacks. These two chapters inevitably strike a somewhat polemical note, as they are founded on my sense that Forster's essays have often been misread and his influence misconstrued. The primary aim of these chapters, however, is less to defend than to explicate, and by that process to restore to Forster something of the importance, both literary and ethical, that has been gradually leached away in the succession of belittling essays and reviews that have appeared since his death.

Nonetheless the polemical is by no means my main critical procedure, which is, rather, at once 'aesthetic', a term defined in *The Princeton Encylopedia of Poetry and Poetics* as the attempt to see the text 'from the point of view of its creator and to reproduce in the mind of the critic the creative process of the artist' and 'judicial' – that is, the interrogating and assessing of the assumptions and results of that process.[8] In Chapters 3–4, I attempt to practise such a programme. I examine the stories both aesthetically and judicially in order to show how they are formed out of a dense kernel of private myths that borrow the colouring of traditional mythic patterns and figures; at the same time I look at their complex narrative structure and the multiple voices and intricate strategies that both carry and conceal meaning. However, the mythic materials that feed the short stories are also present in the historical essays, a form of writing that is closest to that boundary space between genres that I define as peculiarly Forster's own. Indeed, had Forster not early on set out to be a novelist who gave himself the task of continuing Jane Austen by way of refuting George Meredith, he might well have become an historian whose task would have been to refashion Gibbon in the voice of Voltaire, but personally rather than imperially, as an archaeologist of the human spirit, not as a chronicler of empires. The forms this historical exploration took, its relation to Lytton Strachey's writing, and the connections between the historical and mythic imaginations are the subjects of Chapter 5.

Whatever else this book is, it is not a survey of the stories and the essays, a treatment they have time and again received in the obligatory chapter on each in most discussions of Forster's writing, where they are nearly always placed in the shadow of the novels. Nonetheless, the stories and essays are not systematically accounted for in this study either. Many of the essays are not mentioned at all, especially those that were originally book reviews. In the case of quite a few I regret not having woven the net in such a way as to have been able to catch them. But in so far as the net is made out of a specific set of themes – writing across the genres; the transformation of the past; myth and history; the private self and the public text; the creator as critic – and in so far as my touchstone figures are Montaigne, Gibbon and Voltaire, there are inevitably texts that will slip through it or, if caught, will merely repeat points already made. Since Forster wrote far fewer stories than essays, selection was less of a problem, but there too I have concentrated primarily on those that best speak to (or can be addressed through) this set of concerns. The assumption underlying all principles of selection and patterns of argument is that these stories and essays are as worthy of close reading and careful listening as anything else that Forster wrote. They are often infinitely moving, always intellectually demanding, and frequently startling in their reinvigoration of language and their clarity of voice.

2

Writing between the Genres

Forster was always writing. Indeed, the common notion that somehow his pen dried up after 1924 with the publication of *A Passage to India* could not be more false. The impulse to account, recount, tell, meditate, speculate took form daily in diary, commonplace book, notebooks, letters, to say nothing of the stories, essays, lectures, reviews, broadcasts and novels. What identifies all this writing as from the same pen is, first, its open-endedness, its unwillingness to dogmatize or reduce; second, its creation of a voice at once vatic and particular; and, third, its powerful narrative impulse. This does not mean that Forster was primarily a story-teller, weaving experience into anecdote. Rather he wrote as one interested in finding out what he was thinking. This exploratory quality is revealed in his attention to the act of telling, in his awareness of writing as a form of experience itself. But such a statement as 'writing is the experience it records' does not, in Forster's case, imply a writer peering into an endlessly receding succession of mirrors. It does, however, define the text as an open space that is created by the act of exploration. At the same time, Forster seems detached from this process; he never let himself be seduced or tricked by his own verbal skills. The act of going back over his words, checking the worth of the metaphor and the validity of the abstraction, is as much a part of the text as the event, idea, person that generated it in the first place. The text thus reveals itself as process, the writer as reader.

This narrative impulse – to shape an idea and then reflect on the act of shaping – is most evident in the informal writing, but it is also what distinguishes the published prose, particularly the non-fiction. It is not the same thing as attention to craft, although that is, of course, involved. It can, perhaps, best be described as heightened consciousness (but not self-consciousness) of that point where experience, idea, emotion and word intersect. It is a way of writing founded on a sense of the inherent resistance of language, for

Forster was acutely aware of how liable words are to falsify, how difficult the act of narration is, how inherently fictional. Thus all writing is revision: the statement, its action or its testing, and the restatement.

The generic label for the writing that results is 'essay', a term that can apply to the diary and *Commonplace Book* entries as well as to the obvious instances collected in *Abinger Harvest* and *Two Cheers for Democracy*. They are trials in the etymological, Montaignesque sense – short, exploratory narratives in which experience, belief and language are in constant, unresolved engagement. The essay form, I would suggest, was a particularly congenial one for Forster. It was far less constrained than other forms of narrative by conventions carrying a built-in thematics and ideology. After all, no one need marry in an essay. Furthermore, an essay can be all middle, endings being largely a function of voice, and beginnings simply the premise of the 'middle'.

To make such an assertion is by no means to diminish the place of the novels in Forster's total accomplishment. It does, however, provide another means of access to the fiction; that is, it allows us to see the relation, in Forster's case, of the fiction-making impulse to the larger activity of writing. It is not simply that Forster was often an essayist in his novels (especially in *The Longest Journey* and *Howards End*), but that the novels like the essays move from idea to the fictional embodiment of the idea. They do not start with 'story', in the sense that Forster defined the term in *Aspects of the Novel*. They may, of course, start with people; but, then, so do many of the essays.

And, of course, so do many of the short stories. For that form, too, was, in the great variety of its fictional modes, ideal for Forster's purposes. There was no dominating tradition to work with or against; there were no constraining marriage conventions. The short story in England was then so new, so potentially malleable, that Forster could shape it to his purposes with much greater ease than he could the novel. The stories do not depend on 'story' either. They develop it, to be sure – it is unavoidable – but not before a melody has sounded. Because the short story can shelter in the realms of fantasy and prophecy, it need not, like its heavyweight cousin, the novel, be so 'sogged with humanity'. It can, to use one of Forster's favourite words, sing.

However, to speculate on Forster's uneasiness with the notion of 'story' in *Aspects of the Novel*, the 'drooping, regretful' admission that

'Yes – oh dear, yes – the novel tells a story',[1] is to go some way towards identifying what he valued in writing and to make it easier to see why the essay and short story were forms so particularly well suited to his talents. It may well be that this view of 'story' as an atavistic impulse, labelled variously as 'tapeworm' or 'backbone', was coloured by his own difficulties with the purely story-telling part of novel writing. The sudden deaths and coincidences are often identified as symptoms of this problem, the stuff of melodrama if we detach them from their words and cease listening to the 'melody'.

Indeed, none of Forster's novels, with the possible exception of *A Passage to India*, is particularly remarkable for its story. That aspect of writing does not seem to have interested him; it was too much a matter of technique or craft. In a 1912 letter to the Belfast novelist Forrest Reid he makes this clear:

> As for 'story' I never yet did enjoy a novel or play in which someone didn't tell me afterward that there was something wrong with the story. . . . 'Good Lord, why am I so bored?' – 'I know; it must be the plot developing harmoniously.' So I often reply to myself, and there rises before me my special nightmare – that of the writer as craftsman, natty and deft.   (19 June 1912: L&F, I, 136)

Writing is a riskier, less predictable business than the natty craftsman knows. The story may not come out right, but that very failure may indeed be the writing's strength.

The idea that the real business of writing is done below the well-crafted surface was one of Forster's often-reiterated beliefs. In the same year as the letter to Reid he wrote in the dialogue-essay 'Inspiration': 'Perseverance, benevolence, culture, and all the other qualities that pose as good writing, are worthless if they are not rooted in the underside of the mind' (*AE*, p. 121). During writing, he argued, 'a hidden part of [the mind] comes to the top and controls the pen' (p. 119). In 1925, in 'Anonymity: An Inquiry', the idea is developed in the discussion of the two personalities of the human mind – the upper with a name and dinner engagements and 'the lower . . . a very queer affair. In many ways it is a perfect fool, but without it there is no literature, because unless a man dips a bucket down into it occasionally he cannot produce first-class work' (*TC*, pp. 82–3). Again, in his lecture 'The Creator as Critic' (1931, KCC[2]), he stressed the importance of the dream element in all writing, for without it nothing can happen, 'neither "Kubla Khan" nor *King Lear* nor *Wuthering Heights . . .* nor Gibbon's *Decline and Fall'*. Finally, in 'The Raison d'Etre of Criticism in the Arts' (1947), he gave the idea its most quoted formulation:

> What about the creative state? In it a man is taken out of himself. He lets down as it were a bucket into his subconscious, and draws up something which is normally beyond his reach . . . when the process is over, when the picture of symphony or lyric or novel (or whatever it is) is complete, the artist, looking back on it, will wonder how on earth he did it. And indeed he did not do it on earth.   (*TC*, p. 111)

His belief in the connection between creativity and the underside of the mind is connected to the frequent recording in his *Commonplace Book* of 'dream sentences, rescued from oblivion' (*CB*, p. 101).[3] He transcribed collections of words that remained intact on awakening: 'the other man made a noise as if he'd been pickling potatoes', or 'I merely told you the intelligent talk of an important husband' (p. 112), or 'the proud treacherous night has almost puzzled me' (p. 101), or 'have you escaped, sir, the Locked Door policy?' (p. 197), or, my favourite,'The 17000 smells of God' (p. 234). He never elaborated them or speculated on their meaning, recording them, I suspect, in the hope that one day, as happened to Coleridge, the rescue operation would haul up a prize worth the saving. They do provide, however, some glimpse into the odd workings of the 'lower personality' and evidence of Forster's continued interest in its operation.

It is important to emphasize, however, that this lower personality does not just produce novels, poems and plays, but *The Decline and Fall* as well. For the work of art must have its own kind of visionary coherence, in Gibbon's case the meditation 'in the church of Ara Coeli before the Roman Empire could be shaped to his purpose' ('The Creator as Critic', KCC). It is true that Forster never claimed such status for his essays and tales; more often than not he referred to them disparagingly as journalism, and in his suspicion of criticsm he insisted on the distinction, as Virginia Woolf phrased it, between 'the truth of fact and the truth of vision'.[4] But he made two exceptions, and the terms of those exceptions may be helpful in looking for a way to talk of his writing, fiction and non-fiction alike.

Writing in his *Commonplace Book* in 1929 about the distinction between thought and logic, he claims that the former,

> classed by G. Heard as an emotion, has only been serviceable twice, once in a paper on Dante, written over 20 years ago, and once, more recently, in 'Anonymity'. Here there was a process, as of a living thing developing, it was a pleasure to create, and a satisfaction afterwards, and the detection of flaws in my argument left the general cleanliness and beauty unaffected. Why has this noble quality come so seldom to me? After 'pure creation', from which it is separated by a boundary I can't yet define, it is the most desirable quality for a writer, and, unlike pure creation, it ought to strengthen as he grows older. It is impressive without being pompous: that separates it from rhetoric. It isn't the same as thinking things out, which only demands acuteness and pertinacity. It is a single organic advance, not a series of isolated little attacks.   (p. 52)

One should recall here that it is in 'Anonymity' that he develops the idea of the lower personality, although in the passage just quoted he would seem to exempt the essay, but just barely, from the state described there.

Even so, he comes very close here to claiming the status of 'pure creation' for these two essays, especially in the phrases 'a process, as of a living thing developing' and 'a single organic advance', but then he draws back. It is, however, exactly on that borderline that I should locate nearly all his work in the short narrative form, arguing that generic differences count for very little in determining whether a particular text is nearer or further from that anonymous state of pure creation. What they all share is the essential rhetorical procedure that transforms idea into fiction – that is, they begin with a premise that gradually accretes a fiction.

In stories as varied as 'The Other Side of the Hedge', 'Mr Andrews', 'The Machine Stops' and 'Arthur Snatchfold', for example, the generalizing idea is embedded in the story, but it also precedes the story. For, at the same time as these tales are imagined fictions, they are meditative essays on ambition, desire, selfhood, selflessness, lust, history and the law. Indeed many of the stories can be described as metaphors or parables for unwritten essays, in which argument and generalization, rather than containing the fiction, reside more suggestively at its centre. Similarly many of the essays, especially the early historical sketches such as 'Cardan' or 'Gemistus Pletho' and, most strikingly, 'Macolnia Shops' and 'A Letter to Madan Blanchard', as well as several of the cultural– political meditations such as 'Mrs Grundy at the Parkers' or 'Our Deputation', arrive at their statements less through the discursive procedures of intellectual argument than through the metaphoric structures created and inhabited by characters – real, imagined, or both – who act out the implicit ideas of their fictional situations.

Both the essayistic story and the story-like essay have their origins in the nineteenth-century sketch, a form that was quite vigorous and various at the end of the century. There were the popular anecdotal sketches and tales in the quiet ruminations of Cunninghame Graham in books such as *Notes on the District of Menteith* (1895) and *Thirteen Stories* (1900), and in Maurice Hewlett's *The Road in Tuscany* (1895) and *Little Novels of Italy* (1899). There was also the visionary essay–sketch on social and political themes, often using settings of the past, of William Morris in *The Story of the Glittering Plain* (1891) and *News from Nowhere* (1890), and the prose poem of Edward Carpenter, *Towards Democracy* (1883), as well as his travel sketches in *From Adam's Peak to Elephantia* (1892). In terms of generic considerations, however, the most interesting are those essays, tales and prose poems that descended directly from Pater's *Imaginary Portraits* (1887) and *The Child in the House* (1878, 1895). These include Arthur Symons, *Images of Good and Evil* (1899); John Addington Symonds, *In the Key of Blue* (1893); Violet Paget ('Vernon Lee'), *Genius Loci* (1899); Richard Le Gallienne, *Prose Fancies* (1894–6); and, most notably, Wilde's *Poems in Prose* (1894).

However, these texts, although they have something of the vatic, ruminative quality of some of Forster's stories, are, on the whole, more abstract and less completely imagined. Even Wilde's prose poems provide only a slight echo, more a fragrance. Forster no doubt knew them, both because of his wide reading of Wilde (the influence of *De Profundis* on *Maurice*, for example, has been strikingly demonstrated by Claude Summers[5]) and of his interest in French literature (Wilde had adapted a form particularly developed by Baudelaire in *Le Spleen de Paris* [1869], and subsequently used by Mallarmé, Rimbaud and Laforgue). He would certainly have responded to their mildly allegorical manner, their *tristesse*, their method of a theme and variations on scriptural and mythic topics.

'Mr Andrews' (1911), for example, in its dialogue between the

Christian and the Turk and in the scene of the souls before the voice of God, is reminiscent of Wilde's 'The House of Judgement', not just in manner but also in 'moral', for in neither piece is Heaven finally imaginable. Nonetheless, though the elements are similar, the result is markedly different. For all its charm, there is a mechanical quality to Wilde's piece. It generates its ending too simply; as parable turns into aphorism, closure is purely verbal. God confronts 'the Man' at Judgement with his derelictions and abominations and at each accusation the Man replies, 'even so did I'. But, when God at the close condemns him to Hell, the Man replies, 'Thou canst not . . . because in Hell have I always lived.' God ponders and speaks:

> Seeing that I may not send thee into Hell, surely I will send thee unto Heaven. Even unto Heaven will I send thee. And the Man cried out, 'Thou canst not.' And God said to the Man, 'Wherefore can I not send thee unto Heaven, and for what reason?' 'Because never, and in no place, have I been able to imagine it', answered the Man. And there was silence in the House of Judgement.[6]

Forster's parable, on the other hand, keeps expanding beyond closure. For one thing, there is no single assertion that exhausts the fiction. If it is about the unimaginableness of Heaven, it is also about the limits of the human imagination: 'We desire infinity and we cannot imagine it' (*CT*, p. 231). If it is about self-delusion, about the difference between expectation and hope, it is also about human love, the necessary movement out of the self, salvation as a human act. To be sure, salvation is here an idea illustrated, rather than a conclusion achieved against the unpredictable resistances of a daily life which in the novelist's domain cannot be quite so easily disposed of. It is, even so, an abstraction infused with human passion. For Forster, as I shall attempt to demonstrate through this study, it was no passing notion. Several times in his letters, diaries and *Commonplace Book* he refers to it as his constant theme: 'two people pulling each other into salvation is the only theme I find worthwhile' (*CB*, p. 55). Indeed such a statement may well explain why he chose this particular story when he was asked by the BBC to read from his fiction in 1947. For the story illustrates the precept with utter literalness. Each takes the other into Heaven, just as each sees his own disappointment in the other's experience. Both together – hand in hand as when they entered – pass out of Heaven's gate 'and all the love and wisdom they had generated, passed into . . . [the world soul], and made it better' (*CT*, p. 232).

Its suitability as a piece for voice also points to another of its striking qualities. For the tonal modulations to the narrating voice are as subtly nuanced as the ethical conundrums at the parable's centre. This voice is both above and within the fiction: at times it talks of the two souls, at others it joins with them. Even when this joining produces an ironic disclosure of human incapacity – the appropriation by each as an exclusive right of the word 'believer', or Mr Andrews's 'broad church' description of his faith, 'the word "broad" quaver[ing] strangely amid the interspaces' (p. 226) – the result is to enlarge rather than diminish the human actors. They are not quite characters, for this is parable not novel, but they are not the abstractions of Wilde's prose poems either.

This intermediate status in which the human actor both bears and is the signification is found throughout the short stories, in 'The Point of It' and 'The Celestial Omnibus', for example, as well as in the type of fiction I am considering here. However, in all of the stories, even those closest to the Symonds sketch or the Wilde prose poem, one can observe the novelistic imagination at work, locating, specifying and peopling, as well as the historical imagination as it visualizes and reconstructs, and the theoretical and ratiocinative mind, assessing and valuing. And a good part of the pleasure of the text derives from our never being sure which voice, which mode of imagining, we shall encounter next.

More an exploration of metaphor than an elaboration of parable, 'The Other Side of the Hedge' (1904) is, I think, the closest of all the stories to essay. The fiction unfolds in direct relation to an analysis of its meaning. The story is essentially about its vocabulary, its primary action, an emptying of that vocabulary of its catch phrases and false meanings. Like 'Mr Andrews', the story illustrates an idea – the loss of true life (brotherhood, nature) in the mechanical pursuit of a phantom progress – but it approaches it obliquely, in something of the manner of Butler's *Erewhon*, using a naïve protagonist incapable at first of understanding his experience but ultimately converted by it. It makes allusive use of Virgil and possibly of Milton, and, like 'Mr Andrews', plays a variation on the theme of two people pulling each other into salvation.

The wearying race down the road is both metaphor and fact; it is an activity in itself and it stands for the sum of activities that constitute the business of life. Hence one of the runners, Miss Eliza Dimbleby, is 'on the road', due to lecture that night at Tunbridge

Wells. In the same way, the milestone the speaker rests on in the first paragraph belongs both to the allegorical setting and to the 'real world', where such a word signals the inevitable progress that all our pedometer measured activities are supposed to bring. This double-valenced vocabulary is maintained throughout: 'milestone', 'outstrip', 'exhort', 'persevere', 'lead to', 'outdistance', 'advance', 'progress', 'laws of science', 'spirit of emulation', 'waste in production', 'chain of development', 'discipline', 'goal', 'aims', 'struggles', 'victories', 'destiny of our race'. The story is over when this vocabulary ceases to function.

It is through the last phrase in that litany of the catch words of progress, however, that something of a more problematic meaning is suggested, especially when it is read in terms of its surrounding Virgilian allusions to the gates of ivory and horn. While the speaker still imagines that he 'must get back somehow to the road, and have [his] pedometer mended', he is guided to the first gate, 'white as ivory, which . . . opened outwards, . . . from it ran a road – just such a road as [he] had left – dusty under foot, with brown crackling hedges on either side as far as the eye could reach' (*CT*, p. 44). He cannot exit there, however; that way 'humanity went out countless ages ago' (p. 45). But at the sight of the second gate, 'half transparent like horn, and open[ing] inwards' (p. 47), he loses all desire to leave, forgetful of both destiny and race in its punning double sense, and learns as in a dream that this is the gate through which all 'humanity . . . will come in to us' (p. 48). At that moment he realizes that the stranger who is lowering him to sleep is the brother he thought he had lost 'a year or two round the corner' (p. 39).

The Virgilian echoes here complicate the conclusion. The gate of ivory, Anchises tells Aeneas, after revealing the 'destiny of our race' in a vision of the glory and the trials of the coming years in the scene in the underworld at the end of book VI of the *Aeneid*, is the gate through which the 'spirits send false dreams into the world above'. Through the gate of horn, on the other hand, 'an easy exit is given to true shades'. Aeneas' departure through the gate of ivory has always troubled readers, since it would seem to suggest a connection between our subsequent history, the destiny of our race, and false dreams. That would certainly seem to be how Forster read the episode, for from his gate of ivory descends all the dusty folly of our history. His gate of horn, however, opens inward to the gentle landscape inhabited by those whose dreams are true. Read in such terms, the judgement on the life led on the dusty side of the hedge is even harsher; no palm of victory awaits, no glorious destiny.

The generating metaphor for the entire fiction – the road or race of life – is densely allusive as it ranges in the literary consciousness from Dante's and Chaucer's pilgrimage topos to Milton's wayfaring Christian who refuses to 'slink out of the race'. What Forster seems to be doing here is revaluing that metaphor within an argument that suggests the need to abandon the metaphor altogether. For in thematic terms this is a story about leaving the road, jettisoning a false language and finding salvation. At the last, action and language (or the absence of language) converge. The narrator's senses simultaneously sink into oblivion and expand. But what they attend to now are no longer the worn out words of goals and victories, but 'the magic song of nightingales . . . and stars piercing the fading sky' (*CT*, p. 48).

Placing Forster's stories in the context of late-nineteenth-century prose poems and sketches, especially those of Wilde and Pater, is meant to be suggestive only. Forster was clearly interested in their writing and may well have thought of his stories as working the same vein. But, as aware as he was of a certain shared sensibility, he was acutely aware of the differences. Pater could be called 'great', Forster wrote, because he had 'something to say'. But Pater's style was 'too fastidious and involved with no trace of raciness', nor 'could . . . [he] reconstruct other people's lives, he had not the dramatic sense' (n.d., KCC). Earlier, in a diary entry, Forster had talked of 'an absence of vulgarity [in Pater's prose] which is something like fatal' (2 May 1905, KCC). Nonetheless, in the later appraisal he separated Pater from 'Wilde and the aesthetes', for 'unlike the aesthetes he had an instinctive hatred of triviality. He was not content with feeling a sensation: he insisted [and this puts him very close to Forster] on estimating its value.' In some respects, however, his intellectual and emotional affinity was with John Addington Symonds rather than with either Pater or Wilde. In a 1912 diary entry he records, 'feel nearer to him than any man I have read about – too near to be irritated by his flamboyance which I scarcely share'. He then identifies their shared characteristics – education, interests, health, sexuality – and, most important of all for this discussion, 'literary interest in philosophical questions' (10 Jan 1912, KCC).

Not only does that last phrase describe the stories I have been considering; it applies to many of the early essays as well. In them speculation is elaborated through character, incident and scene, and rooted in experience and desire. Although 'Cnidus' and 'Macolnia Shops', for example, are related to the nineteenth-century travel sketch, they have no close analogue in that form for either their blend of experience and imagination or for their shifting the emphasis away from the anecdotal and external to the personal and mythological. Indeed, 'Macolnia Shops' is a perfect example of that 'writing between the genres' that I am suggesting is Forster's habitual narrative mode.

In December 1901, on his first trip abroad, Forster visited the Kirchner Museum in Rome. The visit seems to have yielded one of those resonant moments, like the 1904 visit to Figsbury Rings in Wiltshire, that never diminished in memory and continued to echo in his writing. Lecturing in Italy more than a half century later, about 'the earthly localities where my books were born', he used that museum visit as one of the four or five Italian encounters that had created the experience of Italy: 'There is . . . in Rome, an Etruscan toilet case, called the Cista Ficoroniana with the history of the Argonauts upon it . . . and I wrote about it – the first of many articles.' On this return visit he saw it again, now in the Villa Julia. 'I found it,' he said, 'more beautiful than ever and larger than ever' (n.d. [after 1953], KCC).

That article, 'Macolnia Shops', was published in *The Independent Review* in 1904. It grew out of a somewhat shorter, less formal attempt at recording the experience which he called 'The Museo Kirchneriano' in his travel notebook. It is a curiously moving piece, combining reverie, comedy, travel talk and historical and mythological reconstruction. It has a wide range of stylistic levels, from the Baedeker prose of the opening ('Rome is crowded in the early months of the year' – *AH*, p. 167) to high Romantic prose in the inverted word order of some of the passages of interpretative description ('strong and vivid is the love they bear and have borne for each other') to the social comedy that echoes in the voice of the Roman matron ('I bought the thing because it was pretty') to the meditative historian who holds object, artist, buyer and present-day tourist in a single long view ('It may be that the Greek artist, sitting solitary and content amidst Elysian asphodels, now values that praise more than ours' – p. 169). The essay is constructed out of a chorus of voices: the case speaks and so does the artist who crafted its stand, so does Dindia Macolnia and so do the Argonauts on its surface and the little Pan in the underbrush. Each has a different tonality which sounds through a central narrative voice that allows each its individuality while maintaining its own. Listened to mainly as orchestration, it is a considerable accomplishment.

The essay is interesting both as it describes the process of imagining and as it evokes the thing imagined. Three stories are run simultaneously. There is the domestic one of the shopping of a Roman matron and the two stories that can be 'read' from the decorations on the toilet case she bought. These last two, however, are really two ways of reading the same scene, the more obvious one controlled by the 'motive . . . the Praise of Water', and the second one, 'greater than the first; but it must needs come after it in place' (p. 169), the Praise of Friendship. Whereas the second story takes its coherence from the beholder's vision, the first derives directly from the *Argonautica*. Thus that interpretation is straightforward, a deciphering of the figures based on what Forster knows of the literary tradition. The second has to do with an entirely different tradition, the Whitmanic love of comrades, and is directly connected to Forster's own private myth-making.

What he sees is a remarkably vivid abstraction – the refreshing of the body that leads to a refreshing of the soul: 'when the body is feeble the soul is feeble: cherish the body and you will cherish the soul'. The figures emerge from such a frame. Two stand together, 'leaning on their spears, with the knowledge that they have passed through one more labour in company'. Another is 'pouring water down the throat of a sick friend' (*AH*, p. 169). Forster sees them as emblems of his own desires; they both authorize and authenticate his own artistic enterprise. Their story is worlds away from Dindia Macolnia's shopping-trip. That both are held together within the framework of a single vision is curiously suggestive of the double nature of so much of the fiction that Forster was to write. For in many of his stories and novels, as in this essay, two story lines, a surface heterosexual romance and an interior homosexual romance, are held in tension, much of the energy of the narrative deriving from the conflict between what the plot claims as its main business and what the suppressed inner narrative insists on in the plot's despite.[7] The essayist, however, can move from the one to the other the more readily and, in fact, the more openly. He is, after all, conducting a discursive argument whose emphasis is on the Greek fusion of body and soul in contrast to the later Christian belief that 'in wearing away the body by penance, . . . the quivering soul may be exposed' (p. 169). Thus he can call up a scene and then let it recede; he need not bring it to narrative closure. He has revealed the object, he has recorded the process of creating and re-creating it, and, at the close, can simply return the object to its museum case. But a certain structure has been established, a way of seeing, that remains a constant in all the writing to come, just as the images called up in this first of his published writings recur in nearly all those that follow.

Friendship, of course, was a topic Forster never tired of talking about (nor a state he ever tired of pursuing). Very shortly after the Cista Ficoroniana essay he began work on a story, also in an ancient setting, in which friendship was both the generating idea and theme. The story, 'The Tomb of Pletone', was not published until 1980; it '[went] the rounds' and was put away along with 'The Story of the Siren' (Diary, 31 Dec 1904, KCC). But two years after he first recorded the idea for the story in his diary ('the idea of a story about Pletone, starting at Mistra' – 8 Dec 1903, KCC; it actually ends there), he published an essay, 'Gemistus Pletho', in the *Independent Review*. Looking at the two texts together can be a fruitful exercise, for in this instance the essay both saved and transformed the fictional impulse. What he had tried to imagine in the story, – the episode alluded to at the end of the essay, Sismondo Malatesta's 'great love . . . for Gemistus', a love that defied the Turks as he exhumed the body of Gemistus and carried it to Italy for reburial – did not as *idea* generate a sustained fiction, for it was at the same time insufficiently complex and historically inaccessible. Forster, indeed, acknowledged as much in a remark to Dent in April 1904: 'engaged on the impossible – a short historical story'. The short historical essay, on the other hand, will turn out to be not only a distinct possibility, but, from the retrospect of his entire career, his favoured (and, in many ways, his most personal) medium.

The story concerns three friendships, but the one that presumably prompted it, that between Sismondo and Gemistus, is the one that it is unable to convey. Perhaps the difficulty has something to do with Forster's respect for the materials he was using; he could reimagine them but he could not reinvent them, so that, while the love of Sismondo for Gemistus is a given (he loved him 'as a man might love a god'), there was little to be done with it. His solution to that problem, having Gemistus die before the story begins, contributes to the melodrama of the *dénouement*, but it creates an odd displacement at the story's centre. In place of the historical Gemistus–Sismondo relationship, Forster creates the purely fictional Astorre–Jacobo friendship, which both parallels and absorbs it. However, he frames this with the relationship between Sismondo and Astorre, each on a quest to recover a friend; it is thematically the least important, but, in narrative terms, it is the primary one. It provides our entrance into the story, it generates all the incidents that follow, it establishes the dominant motifs and it conveys the curiously discordant tonality that informs the whole.

Astorre tending the sick Sismondo, for example, oblivious to 'the disgusting and the ludicrous' (*AS*, p. 93), is the arresting opening image. But this scene, it will turn out, is important only for what it reveals about Astorre, his character and his fate. Indeed Astorre is what or whom the fiction is really about, but because Forster never acknowledged this, having committed himself to Sismondo's quest for Gemistus, the result is unbalanced. To be sure, 'stories' do not have to be perfect (we need only remember the letter to Forrest Reid), but this one is at odds with its central intuition. The handling of Jacobo is partly responsible, for he is largely without presence, just out of focus, with the result that the significance of Astorre's sacrificial death is blurred. For that death carries two quite distinct meanings. It is, in part, an oblique comment on Gemistus' failed and absurd attempt to revive the gods of Greece (but as rigid abstractions, deprived of their poetry), inasmuch as Astorre is crushed to death by Gemistus' stone sarcophagus as he attempts to help Sismondo remove it from Mistra. But it is chiefly both the result and the emblem of two friendships betrayed.

The difficulty here is, in part, a result of a collision of modes – the ironic and the lyric – the former devoted to Gemistus' vast project, the latter to Astorre's arduous journey to the discovery, when it is too late, that he must 'found his life on something else'. 'Astorre had seen all his old life die – the life that was founded on friendship. He suffered terribly, for not only had he lost his friend whom he did not cease to love, but he had seen his own baseness and inferiority' (p. 112). It is Astorre, not the narrator, who passes this harsh judgement on his life. The failure of his mission has revealed him to himself: 'like the pilot whom he had drowned that morning, no dolphin would ever carry him ashore' (p. 110). The story succeeds admirably in its evocation of the pathos of this realization and in its suggestion that 'baseness and inferiority' are, at best, partial judgements. For beneath the high drama of the main plot lies a quiet meditation on the value of a love that is outgoing and not self-concerned. In this meditation, far from being a failure, Astorre is the hero.

There is, however, one important link between the two story lines. For crucial to Astorre's portrayal is the absence of fanaticism and the concomitant belief that knowledge is a humane enterprise. Thus, although he may consider himself a failure, we do not assent, given the terms in which the story has revalued the scholarly enterprise. To be sure, he does not survive to have the oratory in his house decorated by Fra Angelico, whereas Piero della Francesca will walk in the procession to celebrate the installation of Gemistus' new sarcophagus in Rimini, and, as Elizabeth Heine tells us in her admirable notes, 'one of the earliest works of Piero della Francesca is the fresco of "Sigismondo Malatesta before St Sigismondo", in the Tempio Malatestiano' (p. 327).

In the only extant manuscript, the story breaks off in a heavily corrected last paragraph, so that it is impossible to know exactly what note Forster intended to close on. Nonetheless, Astorre emerges as an achieved character, more fully realized than the fictional world he is given to inhabit. Furthermore, just as 'Macolnia Shops' reveals a deep structural pattern that informs much of Forster's subsequent writing, so this story establishes in Astorre one of his major character types. Astorre is first in a long line of athletic, unintellectual men who form critical friendships with their scholarly anti-type. Usually the focus is on the anti-type; here it is on the athlete dying young, but in grotesquely unathletic fashion.

The story makes conflicting demands on its readers. We are to give partial assent to Gemistus' enterprise of reawakening the pagan gods, although we are told very little about it; yet we are also to see it as ludicrous and foolish, even tragic. But the greatest difficulty arises from the embedding of this conflict in a fiction of a much different scale, that of Astorre's loyalty and love for Jacobo. There is little intrinsic connection between the two, and the effort to join them does not completely succeed. It is as if Forster could not make up his mind which story he wanted to write, nor decide how to free the historical material so it could develop its own fictional plausibility. It is worth noting that, although at this period he frequently recurred to the idea of writing historical fiction ('the idea of a historical novel, long in my mind, has taken more shape with reading "Thaïs"' – Diary, 16 July 1905, KCC), 'The Tomb of Pletone' and, some years later, 'The Torque' seem to have been his only attempts.

What was beginning to take shape, however, although of this he was probably quite unaware, was the incipient historian. In this role he could put himself into the past, re-creating it as it might have happened, but neither falsifying his material nor himself. Paradoxically the constraint of fidelity to facts in his essay on Gemistus Pletho gave him the space to invent most freely, for reimagining was in some sense a more congenial activity than imagining at this period. Furthermore, this particular act of reimagining touched on a set of ideas very close to his own concerns. When Forster describes Gemistus in the essay as one who 'severed himself from his own church, but . . . did not join any of her rivals', he could almost be describing his own spiritual situation, and even more so in the following assessment: 'Truth, he believed, might be in the past rather than the present. Where his intellectual sympathies lay, he placed his spiritual hopes also' (*AH*, p. 176). It is through such a personal access as this that a character otherwise so remote and so often absurd is touched into the kind of temporary life usually granted characters in fiction.

Despite a certain spiritual sympathy, however, the view Forster takes in the essay is essentially critical. To the degree that Gemistus' intellectual enterprise existed in the story, it was made ridiculous, an empty exercise in classifying gods and demons. It is also seen as absurd in the essay, but more complexly, for Forster is here less interested in the system (it is simply nonsense despite its impressive aims) than in the kind of mind that could commit itself so passionately to such arid abstractions – 'perhaps there has never been a scheme so equally unattractive to the heart and to the head' (p. 185). But, at the same time, 'if he is absurd, it is in a very touching way; his dream of antiquity is grotesque and incongruous, but it has a dream's intensity, and something of a dream's imperishable value' (p. 186).

The essayist maintains two modes of discourse simultaneously: one is epic and philosophical; the other, ironic and dramatic. It is the former that establishes the terms of the argument, a confrontation between civilizations. There the time frame is immense – centuries, millennia roll by, as one moves between the medieval world that Gemistus inhabited and those 'serene plains of antiquity' (p. 176) on which he fixed his eyes; between Renaissance Italy, the true heir of the spirit of Greece, and the dirty, cramped Greece of Gemistus which he tried to make that true heir, all unaware of the futility, indeed the impossibility, of the undertaking. But the essay's primary focus is immediate, dramatic and ironic. In that mode a succession of small, pointed dramas is staged that impose fictional authority on historical fact: disputes over protocol when Pope and Patriarch meet; debates in the council chamber; the conspiracy of a rival theologian and the Sultan's mother-in-law to burn the manuscripts in which Pletho had outlined his extraordinary 'new' religion.

The portrait of Gemistus Pletho that Forster sketches is of a difficult and contradictory figure. At times identifying his point of view with his subject, at others moving as far away as possible, Forster maintains a tensed focus that rests simultaneously on this alien but humanly plausible mind and on the world he inhabited, itself a complex of contradictions and uncertainties. There is a continuous movement between text and context, figure and foreground, subject and self. Although it is not a matter of the writer identifying with his subject (the differences are far more critical than the similarities), that subject is nonetheless constructed as much out of the writer's own experiences and values as out of the 'real' historical materials. It is a relationship between writer and subject that a line from George Herbert's poem 'Vanitie ɪ' suggestively catches – 'he imparts to them his mind'. These words not only describe Forster's method in 'The Tomb of Pletone', but the essential stance he takes to his materials no matter what the genre. From this point of view the distinction between 'story' and 'essay' almost disappears, amounting to little more than the recognition of the relative weight of discursive statement to fictional enactment in a given text.

3
The Stories I: Mythic Fictions

Six months after the publication of *Howards End*, Forster wrote to Edward Garnett about those of his short stories that would soon be published as *The Celestial Omnibus and Other Stories* (1911). 'Do you remember some short stories of mine? I have at last entrapped a publisher into taking them. I am very glad, for I think them better than my long books – the only point of criticism on which I have ever disagreed with you!' (12 Nov 1910, L&F, ɪ, 117). And in the September of the following year he made the point even more emphatically in a letter to Jessica Darling: 'Thank you for what you say about my short stories. I would rather people praised them than anything else I wrote' (24 Sept 1911, L&F, ɪ, 125).

As the letter to Garnett suggests, however, Forster's assessment of the stories was by no means the common one among his friends, whose responses were similar to that of the anonymous reviewer for the *Athenaeum* who found them whimsical and facetious. The vogue for the Machen type of fantasy with an underlayer of mysterious horror hardly interested Bloomsbury (or Forster, although that might not have been perceived at the time), but it may have been an inducement to the publisher. In a letter to Edward Marsh, Forster wrote that Sidgwick and Jackson are 'nibbling, but oh so feebly, and I am afraid that only those to which we refer as "of a mythological nature" will be published' (22 Aug 1910, L&F, ɪ, 115). Even so, this type of story was not a fictional form appreciated by his Bloomsbury contemporaries. Indeed Virginia Woolf later referred to this volume in her essay 'The Novels of E. M. Forster' as 'that curious interlude, *The Celestial Omnibus*' (CE, ɪ, 346). Forster, himself, gave a voice to that kind of response when in *The Longest Journey* he allowed Agnes Pembroke, probably the least sympathetic of all his characters, to demand flatly, 'How could . . . anyone make a living by pretending that Greeek gods were alive or that young ladies could vanish into trees?'[1]

But it is also in *The Longest Journey*, the novel closest in spirit to the stories (and the one that Forster repeatedly referred to as his favourite), that he not only answered Agnes, but also defined the critical difference between the social gestures of the novels and the short fiction's parables, visions and prophecies. There Rickie Elliott, justifying his liking for the unsuitable Mr Jackson, provides the essential metaphor for the distinction. Mr Jackson, he explains, 'tries to express all modern life in terms of Greek mythology, because the Greeks looked very straight at things, and Demeter and Aphrodite are thinner veils than the 'survival of the fittest' or 'a marriage has been arranged' and other draperies of modern journalism'.[2] What Forster was able to accomplish in his fiction (but Rickie only partially and that posthumously) was the creation of a narrative mode in which Demeter and Aphrodite share the same fictional space as those 'journalistic' phrases. The two realms coexist in the novels so closely and subtly that one never has the sense that one has left the knowable world for some 'other kingdom'. But in the short stories not only are both present, but one can find oneself on the other side of the hedge at the sudden turning of a sentence.

If some of his readers found this a baffling or unsettling aesthetic, there were others who did know how to respond to it. Forrest Reid, for example, in his first letter to Forster to thank him for his unsolicited kind words about Reid's novel *The Bracknells*, wrote,

> I remember very well reading it [*The Celestial Omnibus*] last summer, lying on my back in a punt under trees, & how the beauty of everything around me melted into & became part of the delicate beauty of your stories. . . . I liked your short stories more than your novels. . . . But in the novels too, & particularly *The Longest Journey*, there is the same spirit if not quite so clearly revealed. That is to say the visible world is not everything, there are deeper and more hidden things touched on, & above all there is a sense of beauty, both of material beauty & spiritual beauty, without which, I confess, no book is of much interest to me.   (Quoted in Fur, I, 211)

Reid was in part responding to the implicit homoerotic quality of many of the stories, a quality present as well in his own writing but in a far less resonant and complex form. For it is the intensely personal re-creation of mythic materials that gives Forster's fiction its reverberative power, suggestive of those 'deeper and more hidden things' that Reid spoke of in his letter. And it is precisely this power that made these stories of such value for Forster that he 'would rather people praised them than anything else [he] wrote'.

Milton wrote of the 'cool element' of prose, knowing '[him]self inferior to [him]self' in that medium, for 'led by the genial power of nature to another task, I have the use as I may account of it, but of my left hand'.[3] Forster, I am suggesting, regarded most of his novels as his 'prose', written but with the left hand. In the letter to Jessica Darling cited earlier, he made a similar point but with a quite different metaphor. 'But I *have* a tall hat (only used for funerals however), which shows that one can get the best of both worlds.' The world that really mattered, however, was less the 'bright and merry' one of *A Room with a View* than the darker, more vexing world of *The Longest Journey* and the stories. Certainly it was that world that he imaginatively inhabited, while the other he looked at and reconstructed – meticulously, comically, ironically – but essentially from the outside, from the vantage of the observer and not from the vital centre.

In the last chapter I suggested that Forster used the essay 'Macolnia Shops' to authenticate his own artistic enterprise, as it provided both a set of images and a way of handling and organizing those images. The essay 'Cnidus' (1904) carries this process even further, for it is not only a record of an experience, but creates the experience it records. And it is an experience, moreover, that is the centrally generating one of all the short stories – the confrontation with a god who is at once human and divine. In several diary entries from this period he describes the Greek gods from such a point of view. In one he talks of the gods in the British Museum, how each time he sees them 'they are more beautiful and more hopeless. It is simple to say they are gods – down to the bulls going to sacrifice on the Parthenon frieze. But I don't believe gods would make one so unhappy. Up to Demeter and Persephone on the pediment they are human and our perpetual rebuke' (13 Mar 1904, KCC). A few months later, in an entry prompted by an exhibition of Siennese painting, he develops the point: 'They puzzle me these Renaissance portraits: they're much further off than the Demeter of Cnidus who's made of flesh like ourselves, though of nobler texture' (15 July 1904, KCC).

In the essay, Demeter is described as the one who 'alone among gods has true immortality', for 'to her, all over the world, rise prayers of idolatry from suffering men as well as suffering women, for she has transcended sex' (*AH*, p. 172). This is an immortality, however, that is in some sense distinct from divinity; it derives, rather, from her humanity, her connection with human suffering. The goddess who generates such reverence occupies a curious position in the essay, particularly in the creation of the essay, for in a sense she is both presence and absence, the more powerfully there because she is not. For neither in the diary entry in which he first recorded his visit (6 Apr 1903, KCC), nor in the notebook in which he shortly thereafter worked up that description as a first draft of the essay, is she mentioned at all. It is no exaggeration to say that she fills the essay and that the encounter with her is what the essay is about, but it is an encounter that in a literal sense never took place. Forster describes himself in Cnidus, peering at the place where 'the mountain had been scarped and a platform levelled' (*AH*, p. 171), but seeing nothing. For, at that moment while the travellers are wet and muddy before the empty shrine, the goddess is warm and dry in the British Museum, safe in her recess, dusted twice weekly and with a railing and a no-admittance sign before her. Thus the essay is primarily a memoir of an imaginary encounter, no matter how grounded it was in actuality. Demeter is a fiction that both permits and validates a real experience. Indeed she is a double fiction in so far as she goes on to inhabit nearly all his subsequent writing. She appears, for example, as visible icon in *The Longest Journey* in the picture in Stephen's room. She is present, too, at the novel's close and at the close of *Maurice*, and in the mythic sub-structures of the Italian novels and of 'Other Kingdom', and, most potently of all, as the presiding mother deity of *A Passage to India* – Esmiss Esmoor.

The encounter with Demeter is not the only epiphany of the essay. Pan makes an appearance, too. Suddenly, mysteriously, their group contains twenty-two instead of twenty-one.[4] Who is the stranger? The essayist is unsure, for the real experience as he writes keeps resolving into something else. He is left finally with no souvenirs, no photographs or sketches, only the memory's urge to transform: 'I never cease to dry up its puddles, and brush away its clouds.' 'Even over that extra person', he concludes, 'the brain will not keep steady' (*AH*, p. 174). But that extra person never entirely departs; he comes back almost at once in 'The Story of a Panic', and, related to Hermes, he is a presence in nearly all Forster's writing.

Although Demeter occupies an important place in Forster's private pantheon, it is Hermes who will occupy us for the greater part of this chapter, for he provides the best access to many of the short stories. In particular he names an important strategy for making memory the focus of creation, for fashioning what Forster, in his 1929 essay on Proust, called the 'artist's instant', that moment when the artist sets out to be a writer, when 'he must simultaneously recollect and create' (*AH*, p. 98). It is possible that we may even be able to identify the precise image of the god who provided this generating 'instant'. In a marvellous group in the British Museum, a temple drum from the shrine of Diana at Ephesus, Hermes stands beside Alcestis. The S-curve of his body is accentuated by his slightly raised left foot, so that he seems, caduceus in hand, to be urging the group forward. Almost contemporary with the Hermes of Praxiteles, he has the same languid beauty; indeed, he seems even younger. To the left of Alcestis, if, in fact, the draped female figure between the two beautiful boys *is* the wife of Admetus, stands Death, apparently beckoning her forward. His arm broken at the hand, his head tilted slightly back, he is framed by two full-length wings that are raised only slightly from the marble surface of the drum base (much less so than the drapery of the other two figures, more a tracery than a relief). To the right of Hermes, but badly broken, stands another female figure, possibly Persephone. If that identification is correct, she is well located, for the group as it now stands is directly opposite the Demeter of Cnidus (in Forster's day, she was opposite the Choiseul Apollo). Although the mother is now alone on her fragmented throne, her shrine at Cnidus was dedicated to both Demeter and Kore, so that originally a standing figure of Persephone was at her side.

There is certainly no disputing the goddess, but is the Ephesian Hermes across the way part of Forster's active repertoire of images? In the same diary entry in which he spoke of the Parthenon frieze, he described another sculpture: 'that wonderful boy with the broken arm – who I suppose is to be called sugary because he's neo-Attic – [who] stands all the afternoon warm in thick yellowy sunshine. He simply radiates light: I never saw anything like it. Right across the Assyrian transept he throbs like something under the sea. He couldn't have done it in Greece.' To be sure, the figure on the drum that fits this description is Death rather than Hermes, but the two were essentially interchangeable in Forster's imagination, as indeed they are mythologically. One need only think of Mann's Tadzio, in gesture very like this 'wonderful boy'. Moreover, the winged figure of Death is iconographically close to

Eros both as he is traditionally referred to and as Forster imagines
him at the moment of his birth in *The Longest Journey*. We have here a
nucleus of important associations for Forster: Hermes, the beautiful
young friend and guide, particularly a guide to the dead, and young
Death, also beautiful and ardent. A diary entry of 1912 makes the
association explicit, 'I have and hope to keep the power of thinking
of death as beautiful' (quoted in Fur, I, 218). Both are merged in
Eros, who thus becomes a figure of love *and* death. The chain of
associations here is similar to Mann's in *Death in Venice*, and it is
interesting that Mann, whom Kerényi called 'Dr Hermeticus' ('Your
work and your nature represent a revelation of that God'), observed
in a letter to Kerényi thirty years after the story, 'I could not help
being pleased to note that the psychopomp is characterized as
essentially a child divinity. I thought of Tadzio in *Death in
Venice*.'[5]

Indeed Kerényi's analysis of the Hermes figure is particularly
resonant for a reading of Forster's mythic imagination, although
Forster's association of Hermes and fantasy anticipates Kerényi's
analysis by many years. Kerényi speaks, for example, of the close
connection between Eros and Hermes and of 'the eternal
relationship of love, thievery and trade'.[6] He sees the figures of Eros
and Aphrodite as essentially one and emphasises their wingedness
and bisexuality. The Hermetic span, in his analysis, moves 'from the
phallic to the psychopompic', and Hermes is seen, 'like every
trickster', as one who 'operates outside the fixed bounds of custom
and law'. He is a 'hoverer-between-worlds who dwells in a world of
his own'.[7]

Hermes, in Forster's fiction, is both a figure with a name, and a
point of view, a way of seeing and acting. He is one of a trinity of
male mythological figures, and by far the most significant. Pan, his
son, was, for a time, more in fashion, but, as Patricia Merivale has
shown, he had become a relatively trivialized figure by the first
decade of the twentieth century.[8] Although Pan was still important
for Forster, particularly as a figure of sexual awakening, he was too
easily sentimentalized, not as resonant mythologically as was his
father. Even in his most important appearance, in 'The Story of a
Panic', he belongs to a larger pattern shaped by Hermes. Orion, the
hunter, completes the trinity. He provides a recurrent image in
Forster's fiction, a promise of freedom, a vision of the enlarged male
self, the rough woodsman.[9] Both Pan and Orion will figure in this
study, but it is 'the mystifying son of Maia, that enticing divinity

who calls forth ever renewed attempts at interpretation', that must claim our attention.[10]

Neither a heavenly presence nor an eruptive natural force, he is Hermes *philanthropotatos*, most friendly of gods to man. For Forster he is an essential component of the double-sexed spirit of fantasy: 'She or he. For Fantasy, though often female, sometimes resembles a man, and even functions for Hermes, who used to do the smaller behests of the gods – messenger, machine breaker, and conductor of souls to a not-too-terrible hereafter' (*CT*, Intro., p. v).[11] It is this 'lightly built' figure who introduces the stories gathered together in *The Eternal Moment* (1928). Again, some years later, he leads forth the *Collected Tales*. To him Forster dedicated *Pharos and Pharillon*, and he concludes that book as well, as he presides over the descent into the asphodel. Hermes belongs completely neither to the realm of life nor to that of death. His true space – and the one most frequently evoked in Forster's stories – is the space between worlds.

The Hermetic presence is chiefly felt in the shaping of the narrative. He informs the controlling point of view, which is often distinct from the teller of the tale. For the narrators can be dull and uncomprehending, unaware of the story that is really happening on the other side of their narration. For the purposes of this discussion, I shall give that controlling point of view the name 'Hermes' (indeed in 'The Celestial Omnibus' he even appears under his sign) and watch the forms he takes and the tricks he plays. His repertoire of jokes, for example, allows a Tytler or an Inkskip to imagine that he is telling a story, whereas, in fact, the stories they narrate, or the one that Bons experiences (he could have been the narrator except for his nasty fall), do not happen as they imagine. We are witness to a process of transformation of which the teller is ignorant. But their pupils, who become in the stories the poetry their teachers imagined themselves to have read and understood, enter the realm of Hermes – death in the world, rebirth in the spirit.

'The Story of a Panic' (1904) uses the obvious device of an obtuse narrator who is treacherously involved in the story's events, but who is unwittingly instrumental in the triumphant conclusion. Tytler, in his temptation of Gennaro, precipitates the leap that frees Eustace and returns him to his vision of Pan, experienced both as epiphany and human touch. Gennaro is both god and boy, the human evidence of the rapt vision. He is the true shaper of the tale, although as mere actor, corruptible and weak. 'I made the new note crackle in my pocket; and he heard it', Tytler explains. 'He stuck his hand out with a jerk; and the unsuspecting Eustace gripped it in his own' (*CT*, p. 33). Even from the Tytler perspective (although we are not to imagine that he intends any pathos in his use of 'unsuspecting'), there is an intimation of the larger meaning of the embrace. Gennaro, of course, sees it all the more sharply because of his own complicity: 'He longed for a friend, and found none for fifteen years. Then he found me, and the first night I – I who have been in the woods and understood things too – betray him to you, and send him in to die' (p. 35). Ironically, it is through his apparent treachery that he provides Eustace with his only means of escape and interprets that escape rightly as salvation: 'He has understood and he is saved. . . . Now, instead of dying he will live!' (p. 38).

Although Gennaro participates in the Pan myth – indeed, completes what was begun in the 'little clearing' on the mountain – he also performs the function of Hermes in his chthonic aspect. For the 'life' he leads Eustace to is, within the givens of the story's world, death, although the story does not, indeed in its narrator's hands cannot, follow him there. Nonetheless, it is through the narrator's language that such an interpretation emerges. When the narrator, by way of ordering his materials, says, for example, 'but the day was nothing to the night' (*CT*, p. 25), he is only interested in establishing a time frame and generating a heightened interest in the events he is recounting. The statement further functions as part of his characterization in so far as it catches something of his exasperation and confusion. But the line also works allusively, enlarging the moment, suggesting that this is no ordinary day and night, but a metaphor for the entire human span.

The allusion is to a passage from Pindar's Eighth Pythian Ode, lines which, as Furbank explains, became a kind of 'charm or maxim' for Forster. He even inscribed them on a piece of paper which he took with him on his 1903 trip to Greece:

> Man's life is a day. What is he, what is he not?
> Man is the dream of a shadow. But when the god-given
>   brightness comes
> A bright light is among men, and an age that is gentle comes to
>   birth.
>
> (Fur, I, 101[12])

Thus the day and night the narrator refers to in fact constitute the sum of Eustace's life. As he will two decades later in 'The Life to

Come' (although there he will invert the structure, moving from night to evening to day to morning), Forster uses the allusion both to frame the experience and to extend its meaning. The double note of poignancy and triumph that one hears in these lines from Pindar is also sounded at the story's conclusion. 'Signora Scafetti burst into screams at the sight of the dead body, but far down the valley towards the sea, there still resounded the shouts and laughter of the escaping boy' (*CT* p. 38).

In 'The Story of a Panic', Pan's presence is felt as a sudden eruption; in 'Other Kingdom' (1909), by contrast, he is a constant presence, for he dwells, as is carefully glossed, 'most places, as name implies' (*CT*, p. 76). Inkskip, the perpetrator of such useful pedantry, is, in many ways, a more interesting figure than Tytler and less a caricature. He is passionless, neutral, the embodiment of the practical world that Evelyn absolutely escapes from at the end. Those two words – 'absolute(ly)', 'practical(ly)' – construct the story between them. Indeed they are the governing polarities of all Forster's fiction. The world of fantasy exists 'absolutely'; that of reality only 'practically' in the sense both of 'almost' (i.e. tentative, preformed, unrealized) and of 'useful in the ordinary ways of the world'. In the last sentence of 'Other Kingdom', the contrast and the triumphant escape are given visionary authority: 'She has escaped you absolutely, for ever and ever, as long as there are branches to shade men from the sun' (p. 112). It is Ford, whose private joke is to keep a diary called 'Practically a Book', who, in this utterance, becomes the spokesman for the absolute, a witness to a transformation so total that it escapes the world of sexuality altogether. We may imagine Eustace re-enacting eternally the gesture of awakening to his true sexual identity. But Evelyn, in her transformation, presides over just such a pre-fallen vegetable world as the Marvellian lover might have given to his coy mistress had there been world enough and time.

Ford is the primary agent of translation and interpretation, and, like Gennaro in 'The Story of a Panic', is the human evidence of the god. But he is more Hermes than Pan, for there is little of the earlier story's rough sexual energy in him. He is both a repository of mythological and literary allusions and mischief-maker and messenger. Exempt from the consequences of passion himself (his physicality is almost an abstraction; he believed, in Forster's comic phrasing, that his muscles grew while reading Pindar), he provides the literary contexts (Ovid, Virgil, Pindar, Sophocles) for Evelyn's literal translation and becomes its scholar–interpreter. Indeed that role is his from the start as he records her words in his 'Practically a Book' and thus attests to their truth.

One of these statements becomes, in fact, the pivot on which the entire story turns. It records her description of the classics: 'They are so natural. Just writing down things' (p. 89). Her fiancé, Worters, seems to assent, but he makes a fatal change, for by saying, 'it *only* writes things down' (emphasis added), he ranges himself 'absolutely' with those who would split literature off from life to the trivializing and emptying of both. Evelyn's definition is, of course, the true one. In a non-metaphoric way (she is herself all metaphor, which allows her words and acts to be literal), she affirms Rickie's view of Greek myth as a way of looking straight at things. The conflict between these two definitions frames the story's fiction, as it illustrates in abstract terms what is played out on the level of plot. There the conflict is between the cool, almost soulless desires of a human dryad and the greedy, acquisitive instincts of her guardian–fiancé, who, while he might have a vegetable name (Worters) is altogether incapable of vegetable love. Pan might have made his piping music from the reed that was Syrinx, but Worters discovers to his uncomprehending bewilderment that no such solace is available to him (Evelyn's name is also hardly accidental, as it recalls John Evelyn, whose *Sylva* was written about those woods around Abinger that Forster would later celebrate in his *Abinger Pageant*.)

Although the narrator finds Evelyn's definition silly, 'Just writing down things', he still has some glimmers of sympathy for his subversive charges. He is not completely untouched by those books on which his livelihood depends, aware, for example, of the nature of Ford's 'robust dreams, which take him, not to heaven, but to another earth' (*CT*, p. 84). Yet he is a toady, a tale-bearer; his instinct is to trivialize human relations just as he debases the classical style: 'Oh, my goodness! Oh, all ye goddesses and gods! Here's a mess' (p. 97). For him, translation is merely exchanging one set of words for another, whereas the story he tells, but does not understand, demonstrates that translation is in fact transformation. Thus translation, the activity of the story's opening, functions at the conclusion as a metaphor for its accomplishment. 'Ah, witless fellow!' Inskip teaches them pedantically to repeat. 'Gods, I say, even gods have dwelt in the woods ere now' (p. 75). Inskip, this 'witless fellow', thus tells what from his point of view is a story of an odd, impetuous girl, a handsome engagement present, a clever and cynical ward, an indulgent employer. But in the end it is the gods who inhabit the woods whose deed Worters holds in perpetuity, and it is Ford who sees them and speaks their tongue.

The different narrative strategy of 'The Celestial Omnibus' (1908) is the result of a slight shift in emphasis and is more apparent than real. Inkskip and Tytler have been here absorbed into the narrative as Mr Bons, while the nameless narrator plays out a story before his nose which he cannot, indeed will not, see or hear. The story belongs to the boy (it is told entirely from his point of view), although the narrator allows Mr Bons to imagine that, as a reader of books, he is fit to interpret it. It is, for example, the boy's judgement of Mr Bons, 'In short, he was probably the wisest person alive' (*CT*, p. 50), that we hear, although the words are spoken by the narrator as if they were his own. His angle of vision, however, includes both the boy's innocence and Mr Bons's pretentions; it can place the social setting satirically ('after No. 39 the quality of the houses dropped very suddenly, and 64 had not even a separate servants' entrance' – p. 51), and enter, at the same time, into the spirit of the boy's dreams. By the end it withdraws to the ironic detachment of the newspaper account, but the 'end', the 'Telos' – the last word of the narrator before the neutral, external voice of the newspaper – has already been accomplished. For the true objective or aim (i.e. the 'telos' in its primary definition) had been realized in the boy's exaltation.

The exaltation is figured in an extraordinarily resonant image. The boy is caught up on the shield of Achilles and raised aloft, made to stand upright. The shield, as in Homer, is figuratively the entire world, but it is also bounded, shaped, indeed a shining version of that enclosed space – dell, cave, cabin, womb – that figures in almost every story and novel by Forster, and is here made to stand for the transforming power of the imagination. But Mr Bons, unheeding of the words of Dante, whom he has bound in vellum, sees only London and plummets to his death. It is indeed a conclusion of Dantesque tonality. His punishment is to see and not know how to believe, so atrophied has his library-bound imagination become, his fall and mutilation emblematic of his spiritual death.

The story thus records a double journey, the boy's toward enlightenment and vision, Mr Bons's through darkness into death. It is a journey shaped by Hermes, for, as the signpost in the dark alley tells us, the Celestial Omnibus is under his direction. The company, the sign states, will not 'be responsible for any negligence or stupidity on the part of Passengers, nor for Hailstorms, Lightning, Loss of Tickets, nor for any Act of God'. The signature, 'For the Direction', has as its emblem the caduceus (p. 53). As the story unfolds, however, Hermes appears under other names – Sir Thomas Browne, Jane Austen, Dante. They accomplish the narrator's role of witness to the transforming power of imagination as they take the role of conductors to that realm.

These stories move between two worlds. In them Hermes functions as the mythic analogue of the authorial presence, a device that diminishes the necessity for direct intervention, or, rather, turns such intervention into a species of masquerade, where, in the person of the god, the narrator can manifest truths and reshape reality. The short story, in Forster's hands, becomes literally an epiphany. The god himself inhabits there.

But there are two further aspects of the god to be examined: his actualization as the beautiful young boy whom we saw exiled from Ephesus to the British Museum; and his connection for Forster, via his role as psychopomp, with death and memory. In both of these roles he has a ready place in late-nineteenth-century writing. He is Housman's 'merry guide', and related, too, to Pater's Denys L'Auxerrois, although that figure is, perhaps, more Dionysian or Orphic. He leads the *danse macabre* in *Zuleika Dobson* (although Forster did not read this until 1912), but, for the purposes of this argument, he makes his most interesting appearance in Henry James's 'The Great Good Place', a story with marked affinities with Forster's 'The Point of It' (1911).

There is no establishing with certainty whether Forster read James's later stories shortly after they were published, nor is it necessary to argue any direct connection or influence. Using James as a touchstone serves primarily to remind us that Forster was working within an acknowledged aesthetic, even as he shaped it to his own special voice. Yet the resemblances, both of tone and structure, between the two stories are striking. In each the central character recapitulates a lifetime while the other acts as his guide. There is, too, a calculated blurring of the boundary between fantasy and reality. An event occurs that is neither wholly within the soul nor within the world. Where does George Dane go in James's story? Who is the young man who takes over his life, whose voice and face merge with the voice and face of the Good Brother of the dream? 'I just dropped my burden and he received it', Dane tells the Brother as the entire explanation.[13] To be sure, the central experience of 'The

Point of It' seems more overtly allegorical, but the vision of a lifetime leading to death and back to life is vouchsafed to Micky in much the same Hermetic fashion as it is to Dane.

The emphasis in my approach to 'The Point of It', that there is a return from death to life, depends to some degree on an unpublished version, a typescript that contains cancelled passages of considerable help in constructing a reading of the story.[14] For it is a story that has always troubled its readers, who echo the title uncertainly, unable to complete the title sentence. But it originally ended with four lines that were cancelled before publication:

> 'Well rowed', cried Micky to the ferryman. 'Three more and easy.'
> The order was obeyed.
> 'Ship.'
> Harold shipped his oars.

These lines, inasmuch as they imply that Harold does not die, remind us that the sunset with which the story closes locates the same moment as the story's opening. The friends are now returning at sunset to the shore they set out from earlier in the day, and this realization transforms the central part of the story, Micky's life and death, from event to vision.

From this perspective, the story arrests the flow of time. Harold, functioning as Hermes, is the stimulus of a vision that allows both for failure and salvation, death and return. Micky sees simultaneously the probable course of his life and that action or gesture which could yet transform it. Thus, as he is excited by the total commitment to the moment which Harold's rapt straining at the oars signifies, he is able to transcend the mediocrity that would otherwise characterize his life and return in the blazing sunset, having successfully crossed midstream. No time passes at all, or no more than the split second which it takes for the boat, working against the ebb of the tide, to cross the channel.

Harold is at the oars. 'The Ferryman', the cancelled lines call him, but that identification with Charon serves only to emphasize his role as Hermes, an association that Mann also makes in *Death in Venice*, published in the same year as Forster's story. There were many precedents for the conflation of the two names, not the least being Housman's epigraph to 'The Merry Guide'. There the phrase 'Hermes guide of souls' appears; it was subsequently cancelled, but the line from Euripides generally regarded as the source for the quotation refers instead to Charon.[15] That Forster should have merged the two names is no surprise. For, whether his name be Hermes or Charon, Harold remains the psychopomp, the spirit of fantasy itself. He is, however, a silent character, whose function as guide of souls is taken over by the narrator. For it is the narrator who unfolds and interprets the process whereby Micky transforms his life. But the transformation is more metaphoric than actual: *no one dies*.

Thus 'The Point of It' contains two stories; one lasts a moment, the other a lifetime. Even without the cancelled ending, one could maintain such a reading. The framing sunset remains. Moreover, Micky had entered the visionary realm quite early when on the second page we see him transform the farmhouse on the shore into 'a star and the boat its attendant satellite'. 'Micky had imagination', Forster tells us. In his eyes, 'the tide was the rushing ether stream of the universe, the interstellar surge that beats for ever' (*CT*, p. 200). It is within this visionary frame that the rest of story unfolds.

Certainly 'the point of it' would have been less in doubt had Forster not cancelled those lines. However, even in its present form, the story hints at that original ending. The chance of salvation that is offered Micky after death, for example, is oddly linked to that opening scene of the holiday outing. Further, the concluding lines seem to erase the intervening years and return the story to its opening moment. Problems arise either way, however. The narrator, after all, says that Harold has died, and gives no hint in his narration that he is continuing his account in a different mode. It is as if Forster had attempted to rewrite Tolstoy's 'The Death of Ivan Ilyich', but from the perspective of the other side of the grave and in a mythic mode that calls into question the actuality of the story's elements. Indeed, one way of looking at the story is to imagine Micky as a reader of Tolstoy's story in that one instant when the boat hung in the tide, and, as a result of that reading, transforming his life.

The power of 'The Point of It' arises chiefly from the strength of its meditation on death – in particular, its suggestion of the relationship between death and memory. In the story, dying is imagined as reliving, and the pain of death as the pain of the failure of memory. This is made explicit in another portion of the story that was removed before publication:

Ah time, is it not enough to snatch the present? need you ruin the past as well? here is your highest crime against man, that man forgets. Even as a [*sic*] write memories are fading, sweet moments are ghostly in the gathering grey, places and friends are passing from my brain as they have long since passed from my eyes; until in the final twilight even this dimness will be a memory, and I shall remember that once I remembered.

One can more easily guess why Forster cancelled this passage than give reasons for the cancelling of the final lines. The tone is, perhaps, too sententious; the 'a' merges with 'I' in a more than typographical error. The contrast in the published story is certainly sharper without it: 'The shades were silent. They could not remember' (p. 222).

Return is, nonetheless, part of the Hermes myth and Alcestis on the temple drum will shortly retrace her journey, Hermes still her guide. The story, in similar fashion, holds life and death in equal suspension, its driving urgency, the sense that life must be seized, followed even to the gates of death, as if only in that heroic striving can there be salvation. Harold is thus a purer Gerald Dawes, seen more sculpturally, without the crankiness he wore in *The Longest Journey*. And Micky seems, especially from the vantage afforded by the manuscript version, more fit than Rickie to grasp the point of it, to know that he has been in the presence of the god and that, henceforth, his life must be changed.

The god leaves his traces throughout Forster's writing in his many disguises from Puck the phallic trickster in 'The Obelisk' to the angry god in 'The Road from Colonus'. For Forster he seems to be simultaneously a mythic mode, an artifact of unsettling beauty and a psychological reality. As myth, marble and desire, he presides in the tales. He knows more than the mere narrators, although he sometimes speaks with their voices. Mercurial, elusive, he gives the fiction its shape and informs it with his spirit.

He is certainly there several decades later in 'Dr Woolacott' (1927), which can be described as a darker and more passionate version of 'The Point of It'. It is a story that turns midway into myth in Clesant's encounter with Death as the beautiful boy, Death as Hermes. But Death in this story is double-faced. He is not only the 'charming new friend' (*LTC*, p. 89), but also Clesant's wasting-disease, his death in life, the evidence of those social assumptions that deny the boy. (Disease says that the boy 'does not exist. He is an illusion'.) These two versions of death play out a psychomachia over the dying Clesant. Disease, long his intimate ('nor was this colloquy their first' – p. 94) enacts his nature by denying experience, denying touch. The other, indeed a ghostly lover, denies the death in life that disease offers and offers instead life in death. His paradoxical demand is to ask for life – that is, Clesant's life – from the dying Clesant: 'pour life into me', he urges. And so Clesant does – and dies.

The release that brings death is explicitly orgasmic, the partner a boy long dead of his war wounds. The figure that links them is Dr Woolacott. He is an anti-Hermetic figure, however, ironically invoked as 'life's universal lord' (p. 95), while in fact identified with death as disease. He is explicitly the other in the duel with Death as the beautiful boy; nor was this their first combat. For what Dr Woolacott dimly recalls when he sees the dead Clesant at the story's conclusion is a hospital ward and his words 'to a mutilated recruit. "Do let me patch you up, oh but you must just let me patch you up" ' (p. 96). His is a negative presence underlined by his absence from the narrative except as a name until this last page. His absence thus becomes the narrative equivalent of his collusion with Death.

Clesant, on the other hand, is all presence. Indeed, for all that the story is set in the apparently real world of an English country house, it seems to take place entirely within him. He is described as 'barricaded . . . in the circle of his thoughts'. The others appear indistinctly, through a fevered vision. 'They flitted out and in, pursuing their affairs like birds, and troubling him only with the external glint of their plumage. He knew nothing about them, although they were his guardians and familiars' (p. 85). So completely is the narrative space interiorized that specifying details of the story's social reality gradually become endowed with symbolic force as they become absorbed into this internal drama. The violin, for example, which he had been forced to put aside, its excitement too dangerous for him according to his doctor, suddenly starts to play at the moment of his first, incomplete encounter with Death. It is a spectral, disembodied music, signifying release, but also incompletion: 'Always breaking off. A beautiful instrument. Yet so unsatisfying' (p. 93). It is a detail that functions on each of the narrative levels: psychomachia, visionary parable, ghost story.

However, the ghost-story conventions are here so subtly attuned to Clesant's internal situation that they take on human dimensions. There is nothing gratuitous in the deployment of the uncanny; it is neither decorative nor atmospheric. It offers, rather, another way of establishing the Hermetic space, the space between worlds. And it endows the fiction with a sensuality and an urgency not present in many of the earlier tales. These qualities may very well have been what prompted T. E. Lawrence's extreme praise of the story: 'It's the most powerful thing I ever read . . . more charged with the real high explosive than anything I've ever met yet'. (quoted in Fur, II, 149). They certainly are confirmed in Forster's reply:

> Yes I know Doctor Woolacott is the best thing I've done and also unlike anyone else's work. I am very glad it got you. . . . I want to know, among other things, when you first guessed the oncomer was a spook. Not until the cupboard, or before? The story makes me happy. It gives bodily ecstacy outside time and place. I shall never be able to give it again, but once is something.   (L&F, II, 81)

'Dr Woolacott' is a ghost story, but not Forster's first attempt in the genre. In 1905, while he was working on 'The Purple Envelope', he wrote to Trevelyan about his difficulties with it, worrying that it might not work: 'I somehow think I am too refined to write a ghost story' (1 Jan 1905, L&F, I, 62). The result of that early experiment was nonetheless more interesting than its publication history or the critical comment it has received would suggest, although it contains an odd disjunction between its constituent parts and its frame, and a rationalizing point of view that works against its ghost-story assumptions. 'Dr Woolacott', however, has none of these problems. It is genuinely a ghost story and it is certainly not refined.[16]

In many ways 'Dr Woolacott' sums up Forster's achievement in the Hermetic story. Five years earlier, however, he had used several of the motifs, metaphors and structures of this form in 'The Life to Come' (1912), a story that is on the one hand related, through Hermes, to 'The Celestial Omnibus', 'The Story of a Panic', 'The Point of It' and 'The Curate's Friend', and, on the other, through its language and imagery and its handling of the motif of conversion, to 'Ansell', 'The Story of the Siren' and 'The Road from Colonus'. Although 'The Life to Come' is the text I shall examine most closely for the remainder of this chapter, I want to backtrack briefly and approach it from the point of view of these last three stories, since they are so densely interrelated that tracing one motif or pattern inevitably involves a criss-crossing of nearly the entire corpus.

In both 'Ansell' (1903) and 'The Story of the Siren' (1904), books are cast into the water, although the gesture carries a quite different meaning in each. In the first it is a relatively simple plot device for freeing the scholar–narrator from his false burden and, through the friendship of the gardener, Ansell, teaching him how to laugh. The image is slightly complicated by the surrounding episode, for, had the books not fallen from the cart, gardener and scholar both would have been killed. But the irony is not elaborated; it works suggestively in much the same way as does the irony that arises from the subject of the lost dissertation, the Greek optative, the tense of wish and desire as well as hypothesis, the assertion of 'what might have happened but did not'. As Robert Martin has demonstrated, the movement of tenses in the story goes from the past to the future conditional to the continuous present, a process in which 'the former philologist presents philologically his renunciation of the optative for the indicative, of hypothesis for reality'.[17] However, the final image of the fallen book ends the story somewhat ambiguously, for that book is a Greek lexicon, its pages turned by the wind as if 'an invisible person [were] . . . hurrying from one word to another' (*LTC*, p. 8). The image thus suggests a provisional quality to any reading one might derive from the fiction; indeed, the narrative procedure works against fixing meaning, as the very last words suggest. The narrator may join Ansell in hearty laughter whenever they pass that spot, but, he concludes, 'I have not yet realized what has happened' (p. 9). Yet, if meaning is provisional, it is still open. The dictionary's words are there to be shaped, even if the dissertation and the notes for it have all been swept out to sea.

Pages turned as if by an invisible hand, a book falling through the water, are motifs that occur again in 'The Story of the Siren', written very shortly after 'Ansell'. There, however, they function chiefly as a framing device, although they have, as well, a bearing on the story of Giuseppe. They both generate the occasion for the story, by isolating the two narrators, and serve as a metaphor for the transformation the story describes. As the book descends through the water, it expands into fantastic shapes, like 'a piece of magical india-rubber stretching out to infinity' (*CT*, p. 245). Furthermore, this notebook on the Deist controversy, seen magnified under water, becomes 'bigger than the book of all knowledge', a metamorphosis that lends authority to the story's visionary conclusion: 'Silence and loneliness cannot last for ever. It may be a hundred or a thousand years, but the sea lasts longer and she shall come out of it and sing' (p. 258). The concluding image suggests that, when this transformation occurs, the new book of knowledge will be the scripture for this revelation.

Writing a scripture for a new revelation of love is the main business of 'The Life to Come' (1922), which also uses the motif of the book cast into the water. However, in this story it is a voluntary act with far more drastic consequences. As soon as the missionary sees the flower-covered Bible on the floor of the hut which had been the scene of his passion, he hurls flowers and scripture into the stream, attempting, too late, to retrieve the holy book. But there is no sense here, as there was in 'Ansell', that he is freed by his act. Rather it becomes a commentary on his denial of what has happened. For it is the scripture that is freed, carried away by the stream to become part of the 'darkness and beauty' of the night. One can describe the remainder of the story as an attempt to recover that scripture in a revised prophetic language. Like 'The Story of the Siren' it uses a visionary idiom to speak of salvation.

Salvation, or, more precisely, failed salvation, is the subject of one of the earlier stories that also stands in an interesting relationship to 'The Life to Come'. For both 'The Road from Colonus' (1904) and 'The Life to Come' are about the experience of conversion, and, in the figure of the enclosure formed by a tree, both use a similar setting for the experience. But the earlier story doubles back on itself; its second half resists the visionary experience of the first and refuses any enlargement beyond irony. Forster is certainly in his novel-writing element in the concluding breakfast-room scene, when the bulbs of asphodel, the plant of the gods, arrive in a newspaper detailing the wrath of those same gods (the device is similar to the one he used at the conclusion of 'The Celestial Omnibus'). He skilfully maintains the breakfast-room chatter at the same time as he activates a mass of those specifying details that yield the ironic so deftly. Even so, it is only in the first half of the story that one feels the pressure of Forster's engagement with his materials. There he accomplishes a mythic enlargement of the moment without diminishing the social actuality. Mrs Forman, Mr Graham, Ethel are all created out of the breakfast-room materials, but in section I they belong to a larger enterprise which pits Mr Lucas against them in his last attempt to contradict that logic of experience which flatly asserts that there are no 'supreme events', that there is only a steady dying. Thus unlike 'Dr Woolacott', which turned midway into myth, 'The Road from Colonus' turns away from myth to story. The gods are angry, to be sure, but they do not strike Mr Lucas directly. His death in life (from his daughter's point of view, a providential escape) is punishment enough.

Thus in 'The Road from Colonus' there is no consequence to the action, no transformation occurs. When divinity suddenly erupts in 'The Life to Come', however, the consequences are immense. For there the analogue text is not Sophocles' play, but Euripides' *The Bacchae*, when Paul Pinmay as Pentheus discovers the perils of toying with sacred mysteries. This is admittedly a somewhat portentous way of describing a fiction that is, at least on one level, a holy joke. T. E. Lawrence's reaction, for example, was to laugh.[18] But it is a holy joke in which the comic and serious curiously mingle. Although the love that is God is by no means the same as the sexual act in the missionary's hut, it is closer to it than the desiccated suburban Christianity that the missionaries, themselves all wrapped in their 'decent' clothing, attempt to export to naked savages. Pinmay, who is the emissary of the God that is Love, has critically mistaken his role. Like the Worters, Tytlers and the Inkskips of the earlier stories, he finds the revelations of divinity sudden, inexplicable and overwhelming. He discovers that the words he has so easily preached have a life of their own, a life to come. Thus the story demands – in part facetiously, in greater measure seriously – that religion must be true to its word, that words mean, that the opening lines are no idle pun, no merely linguistic or even cultural misunderstanding.

But how to deal with the story's words, how to hear its tone and negotiate its mythic universe as well as its socially dense detailing – indeed, how to read it – are questions that most of the commentary it has received over the last decade has not solved. Although it is occasionally singled out, along with 'The Other Boat', as the best of the posthumously published fiction, most readings still seem to work with inadequate assumptions. Norman Page, for example, claims that Forster 'shirks the question' of whether the love experienced by Vithobai and Paul was 'the genuine article or a momentary indulgence in the flesh'.[19] However, from the point of view I am advancing here, such a 'question' cannot arise, for it depends on a world where human relations have a clock measure, in which the social world in its accumulated detail points to the eternal, but keeps its own rhythm and time. In a fiction which records such a world (most of the novels do, although some more than others),

Paul and Vithobai could fall into love and out of love, that is test the genuineness of the article. But that is neither Forster's manner nor matter here, where instead of clock measure there is mythic measure, a day made equivalent to the life of man.

The story's end is its beginning. The opening moment, which so soon as it occurs is denied, is steadily reapproched through the time structure, which moves backwards from night to evening to day to morning (the story's four divisions). It is a time scheme that Vithobai acknowledges, but not Paul, who is conscious only of the forward movement of the ten years of official time, for since time, he assumes, cannot run back, perhaps that event will stay buried in the forest darkness. But Vithobai knows better. Offering his gift on the eve of Paul's marriage, he cries out when repulsed, 'First the grapes of my body are pressed. Then I am silenced. Now I am punished. Night, evening and a day. What remains?' (*LTC*, p. 76). What remains, of course, is the morning, the death scene, the dawning of the eternal day of the life to come. It is particularly ironic that Paul, the preacher of such a promise, should find this outburst 'meaningless'. He is, of course, unaware of the true direction in which the events of the story are moving. Each action he takes is intended to cancel out the past, but with every action the past is made part of the present, until finally the event he will not name is named and Paul, now no mere spokesman for the God that is Love, becomes the sacrifice to Him. Several religious motifs mingle strangely here. From one point of view Paul is Pentheus and Vithobai Dionysus, the flirtation is fatal, and the god triumphs in his power. From another, Paul Pinmay is both a type of Christ and Paul his proselytizer. The conclusion is thus a kind of sacred parody in which Paul's final punishment is a grotesquely inverted *imitatio Christi*. You don't play games with the gods is the conclusion that both Euripidean and Christian readings provide.

The role that Forster seems to cast for himself in this story is part *trouvère*, the poet of a religion of love, and part Mosaic scribe, offering a new scripture for this religion. If Frederick Crews's description, some years ago, of Forster as one who had 'a theological preoccupation without a theology to satisfy it'[20] is one we can readily recognize, then what I am suggesting here is that Forster was attempting to go beyond this by imagining a theology that was true to the full range of man's longings and desires. This is not, as Page and others claim, to equate sex with love, but to demand a place for the sexual experience in the most serious love of all. It is not a debasement or trivializing of Christianity that results, rather a complexly layered theological fiction whose language and metaphors are at one with its meaning. This layering begins with the first line and is most elaborately worked out in the first section, 'Night'. There the reader is placed in the position of the exegete, interpreter of the word 'love'. We are given at the start four versions of the same event, four meanings of the same word. The first statement uses the language of myth, its terms reminiscent of Aristophanes' *The Birds*, the source for a scene that recurs in Forster's writing, most notably in the vision of the birth of love in *The Longest Journey*: 'In full unison was love born, flame of the flame, flushing the dark river beneath him.'[21] In the story, however, the the tone is less visionary, the moment of birth qualified by the darkness and vastness of the world into which love is born. The second version goes slightly forward in time but then retraces the first in a comic pantomime of guns, servants, noise, confusion. The third does greatest violence to the episode; both its language ('a mixture of missionary jargon and of slang' – *LTC*, p. 67) and its truth are debased. In what is almost a parody of a speaking voice, Paul tells the official lie, or, more precisely, the official truth, rendered a lie by the crucial omission. The fourth version is the first to record what in fact took place. But by the time it occurs it contains the other three, and even this version is mediated, for it is the event as it is recalled, not as it happened; the event as it now contains both desire and guilt, the experience and the denial of the experience. This recessive effect of going back and back over the same event sets up a pattern that the story will continue, first as Paul attempts to look back at his ever-altering 'sin', and then in the working out of the backward-moving time scheme.

It is in the first section, as well, that the biblical style of simple and compound sentences and paratactic syntax is most conspicuous. In the paragraph that describes the fourth version of the birth of love, for example, 'and' is used twenty-two times, piling up to the climax of the last four sentences, all of which begin with 'and'. In the two centre sections, in which the narrator follows Paul and watches events unfold from a point of view close to his, the style moves in the direction of the complex sentence and ironic tone of the novels, but never completely, and at the end of each section, when Paul and Vithobai meet, a modified parataxis returns. The final section reverts to the syntax of the opening: 'And confusedly, and with many changes . . . and shiftings . . . and reservations . . . and its present consequences' (p. 79). Then, of course, there is that threefold repetition of 'who calls me?' at the close (pp. 78–80).

I do not know if one can decide absolutely if this language succeeds or fails. Taste, notions of decorum, just plain notions, all may skew our response. But it is important that we attempt to determine what Forster was doing and not prejudge the result. To be sure it is a difficult voice to control – Page dismisses it as 'inflated'; Alan Wilde calls it 'poetic by intention, but . . . flat, thin' in its effect[22] – but such comments seem to me to miss the point, for the language here is directly a function of the materials. If the story attacks a Christian orthodoxy that has platonized and disembodied its sacred metaphors, it does so by way of offering a reconsecrated language and theology that are sufficiently inclusive to contain all human experience. It is a notion of inclusiveness best illustrated by the remark in *A Passage to India* that attempts to explain Hamidullah's inability to understand Adela's honesty and sense of justice: 'How indeed is it possible for one human being to be sorry for all the sadness that meets him on the face of the earth, for the pain that is endured not only by men, but by animals and plants, and perhaps by stones.'[23] That same idea had been phrased a few years earlier, in *Alexandria: A History and a Guide*, 'We're all part of God, even the stones.'[24] In 'The Life to Come', it takes a paradoxical form that is almost Donnean in its physical punning on sacred matters: 'Love's mysteries in souls do grow,/But yet the body is his book'; or, more extravagantly still: 'Full nakedness! All joys are due to thee. / As souls unbodied, bodies unclothed must be.'[25] For neither Forster nor Donne do we have to choose between tenor and vehicle. The story *is* its language; there is no prettying-up process going on, no merely being 'poetic'. And the conclusion offers no gratuitous bit of violence either, but a final spending of all the energies that have built up through the story. From the moment of that ejaculatory sentence, 'and he stabbed the missionary through the heart' (p. 81), there is a strengthening of voice and a quickening of tempo. The earlier figure of the leap of Vithobai from the cart ('his soul uncoiled like a spring' – p. 75) is completed in the final sentence of the plummet from the parapet, half in this life, half in the next.

Thus, both in its imitation of biblical language and in its realization of biblical metaphor, the story objectifies its content in its preaching of a new scripture in a new language. One way of describing the theological matter of this new scripture is as the testing of Christianity from the Indian point of view from which nothing can be excluded. Although it is a testing in which Christianity is found wanting, Indian religions, much on Forster's mind at this time, are not offered as conclusion either. For this story, even more than *A Passage to India*, is religiously syncretic. Its presiding deity is a rather Dionysian Christ and the life to come that both protagonists approach at the story's end is as much Vithobai's 'solid and eternal . . . kingdom of the dead' (p. 82), where he will once again be king, as Paul's Christian Heaven where master and disciple will meet in true spiritual knowledge.

There is an important private dimension to the story as well. Identifying it returns us to Hermes and the starting point of this argument. In a letter to Sassoon, Forster wrote that 'The Life to Come' embodied 'a great deal of sorrow and passion that I have myself experienced' (L&F, II, 45), referring, in particular, to the dismal death by tuberculosis of his Alexandrian friend Mohammed el Adl. In a notebook in the form of a 'letter' to this dead friend Forster wrote, 'I have written a story ['The Life to Come'] because of you and have dedicated a book to you.'[26] The dedication of which he speaks is to *Pharos and Pharillon*; it reads, 'Hermes Psychopompos', for that is the role he is cast in in that book, as we shall see in Chapter 5. In the story, however, the psychompompic motif is more complexly and ironically embedded in the closing episode. For it is Paul who plays that role for the now-victorious Vithobai, who 'swoop[s] like a falcon from the parapet in pursuit of the terrified shade' (*LTC*, p. 82). A diary entry in 1922 along with Forster's letters to Florence Barger help to explicate the autobiographical aspect of this moment: 'All that is satisfactory [he is discussing the difficulty of holding Mohammed in memory] is "The Life to Come" where my indignation found an outlet through my art' (KCC). It is an indignation that was directed against the Pinmays and their missions and institutions, which Forster held responsible for the terrible sequence of events that led up to Mohammed's sickness and death, just as they lead to Vithobai's in the story. The most personal element in the story is thus transmuted into the most public – the death of a beloved yielding a powerful analysis of the ways in which a society can be corrupted and, indeed, made to die.

4

The Stories II: Narrative Modes

To speak of the narrative voice 'as Hermes' is to use a metaphoric language that conflates intrinsic and extrinsic critical procedures, a language that is simultaneously within and outside the discourse it is exposing. This is, however, an approach that Forster's short fiction seems particularly to require. For with a Forsterian text an exploration of the ways in which autobiographical materials are rendered mythic becomes of necessity a discussion of narrative modes and generic choices. Hence a discussion of narrative layers, texts and sub-texts, surface plots and inner plots will involve a certain degree of going back over ground covered in the last chapter, but with a somewhat different emphasis. My primary concern here will be linguistic and structural, focusing on the relationship of a narrative to the words that constitute it, to the speaking voice that utters it and to the writing author who ultimately shapes it.

The assumption that grounds this discussion is that Forster's stories are complex fictions whose significance and accomplishment are far from exhausted by identifying their mythic materials. Indeed, it is precisely because they are strong fictions and not, as they have too often been considered, juvenilia or whimsical exercises in turn-of-the-century Hellenism, that they can sustain an inquiry directed at identifying their multiple levels of meaning and the strategies invented to present (or conceal) these meanings. In a Forsterian narrative several stories are proceeding simultaneously – that is, one set of words may 'tell' several stories, or, alternatively, the story may exist apart from the words that tell it. Nearly all the stories, moreover, have some form of double structure and participate in two or more genres or modes – story/essay, story/novel, fantasy/realism, homosexual romance/heterosexual romance. This doubleness in part results, as we saw in the last chapter, from Forster's development of a complex narrative voice that enlarges the story beyond the primary narrator's comprehension. It is also related to the creation of a voice that functions as a filter for other voices, and it is most interestingly related to a structural pattern that situates meaning in the gap between the overt and covert text.

A passage from 'The Road from Colonus' offers a suggestive text for these concerns. The group of travellers is in ecstacies about the beauties of the grove but Mr Lucas finds their enthusiasm 'superficial, commonplace'. He tries to explain his own feelings:

> I am altogether pleased with the appearance of this place. It impresses me very favourably. The trees are fine, remarkably fine for Greece, and there is something very poetic in the spring of clear running water. The people too seem kindly and civil. It is decidedly an attractive place.   (*CT*, pp. 131–2)

Not surprisingly, one of the others calls his words 'tepid praise'. They all join in, full of their literary enthusiasms: it is just like the Colonus of Sophocles they exclaim; Ethel is Antigone, and, of course, Mr Lucas is Oedipus; these two must stop for a week at least. Of course, none of them means a word of any of this – except Mr Lucas. For him, words may be inadequate counters for his experience, for that sense of clarification, that feeling of continuity and presence he had met in the hollow of the tree. But inadequate as they are, they point to that experience; they carry an irreducible minimum of meaning. What the scene makes painfully clear, however, is that this minimum can be as readily baffled by words as communicated by them, and that it is as difficult to be an adequate narrator of one's experience as a reader of another's narrative (the other characters are all, of course, false readers, first of Sophocles' play and then of Mr Lucas's 'story').

There are thus two distinct functions embedded in Mr Lucas's role. As a mythic character, he is presented as one who has lost his 'moment', defeated by his daughter and Mr Graham, his 'supreme event' nullified as water and children become the substance of his querulous complaints, not the source of his rejuvenation. But as a narrator of that experience he retains his integrity to the end, summing his diminished experience as he had summed that supreme event: 'I shall write to the landlord and say, ''The reason I am giving up the house is this: the dog barks, the children next door are intolerable, and I cannot stand the noise of running water'' ' (p. 143).

Within the fiction, each of his narrative attempts, from the point of view of the other characters, is a failure. His 'tepid praise' hardly prepares the enthusiasts for his belief that he and his daughter were indeed to spend a week at the khan, that 'he would be a fool . . . if he stirred from the place which brought him happiness and peace' (p. 135). And his letter to the landlord is only so much babbling to the distracted ears of his soon-to-be married daughter. The story's narrator, however, affirms these attempts, no matter if they have failed. His narrative, in fact, is the successful version of Mr Lucas's failed efforts. But the poignant incapacity of the sub-narrator puts even that competent voice in jeopardy as it signals the disjunction between story and words on the one hand, words and meaning on the other.

The story that makes such disjunction its explicit concern is 'The Curate's Friend' (1907), although that text usually enters discussions in terms of its variations on the Pan motif. But what is most interesting about its handling of that motif is the way it makes it emblematic of the essential doubleness of fiction, a doubleness that is also duplicity in terms of the story's generating metaphor of the curate's bewitchment by and subsequent happy life with the to-everyone-else-invisible faun. This doubleness is given a specifically generic definition in the story's concluding sentence:

> Therefore in the place of the lyrical and rhetorical treatment, so suitable to the subject, so congenial to my profession, I have been forced to use the unworthy medium of a narrative, and to delude you by declaring that this is a short story, suitable for reading in the train.   (*CT*, p. 124)

That is, to delude you, the reader, into thinking this is a story about fauns. The subject is poetry ('that evening, for the first time, I heard the chalk downs singing to each other across the valleys' – p. 123); the medium is prose.

Using prose is indeed what the story is about – that is the curate's adoption of the necessary strategies for survival so that he can remain 'an asset to [his] parish, [instead of being] . . . an expense to the nation' (p. 124). Bursting into song is as dangerous, the curate senses, as declaring the truth about his present life. Both readers and parishoners require the delusion of narrative. Whereas Mr Lucas is not conscious of the gap between his words and his listener's understanding, the curate certainly is and thus constructs his account in such a way that vision and epiphany can be flattened between the covers of a book 'suitable for . . . the train' (Claude Summers nicely points out the comic allusion here to Gwendolen Fairfax's diary in Wilde's *The Importance of Being Earnest*[1]). A whole range of potential readers is thus satisfied, from the amateur geologist interested in mapping the chalk downs to the train travellers who keep up with their reading enough to know that fauns are in fashion this year.

Not only are there several audiences, but the speaker's voice is multiple as well. At the centre of the story there is the conversation between the narrator and the faun, the voices closest to lyric for the undeluded reader, but they are contained by a prosing narrative voice that comically illustrates its own dullness. In this voice, the narrator chatters on about his preference for a countryside that is 'snug and pretty', how he had turned away from the 'great sombre expanses' that the view revealed 'as soon as propriety allowed and said "and may I now prepare the cup that cheers?"' (pp. 116–17). But this demonstration of how he had 'presented the perfect semblance' (p. 114) of a fool in the unawakened torpor of his life before the faun, comes through a narrative voice that has already completed the process of correction and transformation (hinted at in such phrases as 'in those days'). For this narrator the gap between words and meaning is a necessity in his relation to his audience, but it also allows for the comic misunderstanding of the confrontation scene and is thus necessary for the readjustment of all internal relationships that constitute the story's peripeteia. 'Miscreant . . . you have betrayed me', shouts the curate to the faun, as he bursts upon the scene where his fiancée and the friend who had accompanied them on this eventful picnic are embracing. (The setting on Box Hill is an even more topsy-turvy and chaotic scene than was staged in *Emma*.) The friend naturally assumes that he is the one addressed and responds in comically inflated terms: 'I know it: I care not. . . . You are in the presence of that which you do not understand' (p. 121). But in moments the reversal is complete. There has been no betrayal at all and it is the friend who has not 'understood'. The curate's subsequent protestations dwindle rapidly away, and, as earlier, in 'Ansell', the moment of release comes when he is able to laugh.

Thus, at its conclusion, 'The Curate's Friend' provides a happy, albeit somewhat subversive, revision of the earlier 'Albergo Empedocle', a story whose main character does indeed end up as an 'expense to the nation'. It also offers a partial reversal and then extension of 'A Story of a Panic'. Its most important affinity, however, is with *The Longest Journey*, which was not only published in the same year but similarly used the Wiltshire setting as an imaginatively generating, mythic space. For the kind of narrative that the story proposes, poetry disguised as prose, is precisely that of the novel – indeed, provides in miniature a model for reading the novel. Like the story (and like the early essay 'Macolnia Shops', discussed in Chapter 2), *The Longest Journey* maintains a double story line, a surface heterosexual romance in counterpoise with an interior homosexual romance, and it is from the tension between surface story and suppressed inner narrative that both novel and story derive much of their energy. The story, however, dissolves the tension in its happy ending, and in this way it is closer to the essay than to the novel. Since the story characters can simply bear the ideas out of which they were constructed, resolution can be achieved on an essayistic rather than on a fictional level; statement is sufficient.

The sort of doubleness I am discussing, observable throughout Forster's writing, is visible in its most schematic form in 'The Obelisk' (1939). There the resolution of the double structure takes the form of a good joke consummately well timed and delivered. In that story the two 'romances' are literally played out together. The wife's story (the heterosexual romance) and the husband's story (the homosexual romance) contain the same characters, setting, events and words. But the stories absolutely oppose each other and, because the wife's story finally includes the husband's (she realizes what must have happened; he does not), the comic punch line turns on itself and both wife and reader are left with an awareness that the laughter cannot quite displace.

The story, however, that presents the most complex investigation of doubleness, both on the level of plot and characterization and on the level of narrative procedure (i.e. the disposition of the story's elements and the narrator's relation to his materials) is 'The Other Boat'. It is a story that doubles back on itself and replays itself. Indeed the actual writing was itself a replaying, a taking-up of earlier work and changing it, not by rewriting but by resetting it, thereby both reinterpreting and re-creating it.

The original pages were written sometime in 1913 while Forster was working on *Arctic Summer*, and were most likely intended as an exploration of the early life of one of the two main characters, Clesant March (the names shift from fragment to fragment; in the story he is Lionel). Although the entire project was shortly abandoned, these pages may have hastened that process, since the direction they point in is quite different from that of the other extant fragments. The novel that had already begun to take shape was centred on the 'antithesis between the civilised man, . . . and the heroic man'.[2] 'The Other Boat' fragment, by contrast, pits heroism against fate and cunning, the real against the unreal, the known against the unknown, and it does so in terms that could have had no outlet in the novel as it then stood. With that impasse it is no wonder that Forster put the whole project aside.

The title under which those pages were published thirty five years later, 'Entrance to an Unwritten Novel', might better have been 'Exit from . . . '. By freeing them from their *Arctic Summer* matrix, Forster simultaneously proposed a complete fiction, for there is a form of closure, at least of enclosure, in the figure of the chalk circle which seems to enfeeble Mrs March as it empowers Cocoa, and the possibility of an entirely new beginning. The new story, finished around 1958, in many ways draws together the whole of Forster's *oeuvre*, and is particularly related to two important writing projects of that 1948–58 period, the rearranging and editing of his Indian letters for *The Hill of Devi*, and the writing of the libretto for Britten's *Billy Budd*. The former certainly brought back the Anglo-Indian world of privilege and power suggestively and dangerously embodied in the story by the Arbuthnots and Mannings; the latter provided a focus for the quasi-mystical conclusion, at once tragic and transcendent.

The story proposes an interesting symmetry between the act of writing and the subject of the writing. Just as the writer, in fact, recovered his past efforts and went back over his material, his two characters are similarly engaged in a process of repetition, a reliving of an earlier set of events. The voyage home of the first section is now a voyage out; saloon deck and forecastle have become upper deck and cabin; playing at soldiers – in particular, playing at dying – has ceased being a game and Death is no longer acting.

The world Forster sets out in the story is at once completely self-contained (the ship) and utterly divided, its two characters, Cocoa and Lionel, the human embodiments of this configuration. Cocoa, from the moment he entered the chalk circle, becomes a unitary figure, his power totally deriving from the self, exempt from all contingency ('the door shut, the door unshut, is nothing, and is the same' – *LTC*, p. 189). But Lionel is a completely split figure (a point that James Malek demonstrates in Jungian terms[3]); in him there is no mediating space, no possibility of compromise. Deck and cabin worlds are thus analogues of the split within, of the knowledge of self masked by the lie of self, that leads inevitably to violence and death. A reader may be uneasy with the violence of the conclusion, but it is neither arbitrary nor gratuitous, for it is the only means of bridging the fatal split in Lionel. Thus the union allowed can occur only after death, both with the mother, as she is a figure of the sea itself (Lionel had communed with her/it moments before the last encounter), and with the lover when Cocoa's body moves northward against the current, the undertow carrying it toward Lionel.

Thus both the structure of the story and the history of its composition enact its central thematics of separation and closure. But one of the curious features of the story is that closure is achieved in the symbolic mode, whereas separation, fissure are proposed in the realistic mode. The manipulation of these two essentially antithetical modes gives the story its extraordinary edge, for each event has its daylight and its dark side. Thus the highly detailed foreground action – the deck-life rituals of bridge games, drinks and sleeping arrangements – is made part of a larger, essentially mythic action in which the journey out is felt both as descent into Hell and ecstatic, mystical release. The figure that links the two modes is the mother; at the start a 'character' in the conventional sense, she is pure symbol at the close.

The story opens on a journey home from India, where, from the mother's point of view, relationships do not matter, for the boat world is taken to be unreal. But it is precisely the so-called unreal relationship, that between Lionel and Cocoa, that the story realizes, while the mother's world turns into shadow as she is doubly deserted, first by a husband gone native, and now by her son, a scandalous suicide in the Red Sea. Although a felt presence throughout the story, she is a purely negative creation, a dimmer, indeed inverted, version of Mrs Moore, whose death and burial at sea provide the paradigm for the mother–sea association in Forster's writing. Yet she understands the story better than the others; she can reconstitute it from its partial narrations, from Colonel Arbuthnot's letter after the fact, from Lionel's transparent letter beforehand. Both these letters omit our 'story' completely; together they compose it through their silence. But the story is entirely consumed in her reading: 'and she never mentioned his name again' (p. 197).

However, Forster plays that reading against another. For, if Mrs March's reading denies the story, the crew's response to the burial of Cocoa affirms it:

> There was a slight disturbance at the funeral. The native crew had become interested in it, no one understood why, and when the corpse was lowered were heard betting which way it would float. It moved northwards – contrary to the prevailing current – and there were clappings of hands and some smiles.   (p. 196)

The echoes of the close of Melville's *Billy Budd* are striking, especially those moments in the earlier text which describe the crew's rapt attention, their involuntary 'resonant sympathetic echo' of Billy's benediction to Vere, the 'murmurous indistinctness' of a sound like a mountain torrent arising from the men that 'seemed to indicate some capricious revulsion of thought or feeling', and the final 'strange human murmur' as Billy's body slid into the sea, 'blended now with another inarticulate sound proceeding from certain larger sea fowl . . . circling it low down with the moving shadow of their outstretched wings and the croaked requiem of their cries'.[4] This almost dumb sympathy is given voice in the epilogue ballad, 'Billy in the Darbies', composed by one of Billy's own watch, 'gifted, as some sailors are, with an artless poetic temperament'.[5] It is a view, however, that Melville ironically qualified by the complex shifts in perspective at the novel's close. In Britten's opera, the ballad becomes Billy's aria before the execution. In his visionary acceptance of his fate, Billy there anticipates Vere's concluding aria, in which he recognizes how Billy's death has redeemed him.

There is certainly no consensus on how to read the close of Melville's novel, even whether to see it as hopeful or despairing; the opera text, however, is far less problematic. It makes Vere the hero, despite Forster's sense, expressed elsewhere, that the hero was Billy,[6] and it turns Billy's death into a necessary sacrifice, thus reinforcing Vere's humanity in its promise of redemption. In such a strongly Christian reading, the death becomes a moment of triumph rather than defeat: 'He has saved me, and blessed me, and the love that passeth understanding has come to me.'[7]

Our prior assumption that Forster would not have committed himself to so thorough-going a Christian enterprise certainly creates difficulties in assessing his participation. Although there is both internal and external evidence to suggest that Forster's reading was in part at odds with Britten's, he certainly shared something of the same mystical inclinations.[8] Thus the opera's movement towards transcendence, its other-worldly resolution, may very well have echoed in his mind in reworking his early story. In 'The Other Boat' he both corrects and vindicates his earlier misreading of Melville, for it is in some such mystical terms as I have indicated that Forster set the closing, uncanny moments of that story. The solace he allowed his characters, however, was not that of a Christian consolation, but of a *Liebestod* (to borrow another literary–musical analogy). At the same time he continued to direct his irony toward the ship-deck world where propriety and decorum maintain their sway. His crew does not break into song, but there is a similar note of celebration in their response to the lovers' fate.

Yet, despite this almost mystical conclusion, 'The Other Boat' remains one of the most novelistic of Forster's stories (second only to 'The Eternal Moment', although that story was once described by Edith Sitwell as 'the most horrifying ghost story' she had ever read [30 Mar 1928, KCC]). Indeed, except for the final detail of the body moving against the current, nothing that happens is strictly inexplicable. But, as in many of the stories, everything seems immersed in some other element, making the story world at once magical and real. This mingling of the real and the fantastic is, as we have seen, a marked characteristic of much of Forster's writing. But it is less a literary device in its own terms than a direct function of the double plot structures that I have been discussing in this chapter. The fantastic, for Forster, identifies not so much a separate genre, or even a mode within a genre, as a tonal variable, a means of modulating a set of simultaneous narratives within a fiction.

It is a procedure that goes back to his earliest writing, although he would not have acknowledged it at the time. Indeed, his account in the twenties to the Memoir Club of 'The Story of a Panic' is particularly enlightening in this regard. It is an amusing anecdote in which Keynes rushes to Forster with the news of his friend Charles Sayles's reaction to the story:

He showed Maynard what the story was about. ~~Buggered~~ Corrupted by a waiter at the Hotel, Eustace commits bestiality with a goat on that valley where I sat. In the subsequent chapters he tells the waiter how nice it has been and they try to b. each other again. . . . It seemed to him [Maynard] great fun, to me disgusting. . . . In after years I realized that in a stupid and unprofitable way he was right and that was the cause of my indignation. I knew as their creator that Eustace and the footmarks and the waiter had none of the conjunctions he visualized. I had no thought of sex for them, no thought of sex was in my mind

but, he acknowledges, the sex was there implicitly (KCC). Indeed, he went on to say that there were other passages in his early writing where more was going on than he could have recognized at the time but that such moments had become rarer now that he was older, 'and the clouds [have] lift[ed] from that enchanted valley where beauty is lust, lust beauty and neither has nor needs to have a name'. For the blurring of these terms, fantasy offered both a convenient vocabulary and a suitable disguise.

Furbank, from the perspective of the biographer, remarks how liberating an experience the writing of the story must have been for Forster, as it expressed Forster's own 'feelings of standing in the sunlight at last and possessing his own soul' (Fur, 1, 92). Nonetheless, within the fiction neither author nor creation seems fully to comprehend what has been unleashed. For, if the author was not completely in touch with the sub-plot of his own story, Eustace passes through the pages as a character only in spite of himself. Although the centre of the text, he decentres it by his silence. All the other characters are concerned with interpreting his actions, with reading him. But he takes his actions and his pre-language ('a strange loud cry, such as I should not have thought the human voice could have produced' – CT, p. 38) and simply leaves the story. What comes to conclusion, as a result, is the telling, not the told. For, in so far as Eustace equals the told, the story absolutely resists closure. On the other hand, the story as Mr Tytler's telling is complete – the parodied Christian elements of betrayal, the thirty talents, death and rebirth closing it off even more completely than the account of his own complicity in the *dénouement*. Thus closure is verbal, the using-up of the story's language, rather than narrative, the exhaustion of the predicated experience.

Although 'The Story of a Panic' obviously uses several of the devices of fantasy – the strange footprints, a sudden demonic irruption, an ambiguous conclusion – it is primarily the narrator, in his meticulous documenting of what he imagines himself to have seen, who supplies what Todorov considers the precondition of the fantastic: 'that hesitation experienced by a person who knows only the laws of nature, confronting an apparently supernatural event.'[9] But, unlike the writer of fantasy, Forster is not really interested in that 'hesitation', for the fantasist's aim, to authenticate the unreal or supernatural, is not his. Rather than emphasize the otherness of the supernatural experience, he dwells on the otherness of the natural. There is a blurring of boundaries, but in this story, which develops a poetics of desire rather than of fantasy, it is the object of desire that is blurred rather than the boundary between the real and the unreal.

It is worth recalling Edith Sitwell's odd reaction to 'The Eternal Moment' in this connection. For what she identified in describing it as 'the most horrifying ghost story' she had ever read, is precisely this sense of the otherness of the natural, where the uncanny is firmly fixed in the quotidian yet liable to sudden eruption. Indeed, one way of describing the central event of that story is as an encounter with a ghost, the 'dead' lover, Feo, now materialized as the stout and greasy concierge. The encounter is terrifying in so far as it is this 'ghost' that defines the present reality. But it is a displaced reality, for what seems real is the result of a fiction, has, in fact, its origins in a fiction. (It was the success of Miss Raby's novel that both made and unmade the village, creating its ghastly/ghostly present.) Here, however, the uncanny evolves from within; it is both a form of heightened seeing and a means of redefining reality: 'In that moment of final failure, there had been vouchsafed to her a vision of herself, and she saw that she had lived worthily' (*CT*, p. 307). There is not, as there is in 'The Story of a Panic', an intrusion from without. But 'The Eternal Moment', like that story of the previous year, also depicts the triumph of solipsism. In fact, reading it in the context of 'The Story of a Panic' and 'The Road from Colonus', particularly in terms of its handling of the final moments of vision, clarifies the endings of all three stories. Here the writer–heroine wills the unreality of the other characters as she triumphantly re-enters her own fiction. She is not a failed narrator like Mr Lucas. Although it may seem as if she had lost her moment those years ago on the hillside, she is able now to restore her fiction and render her moment 'eternal'. Thus at the story's end she is far closer to the position of Eustace than to Mr Lucas. The 'shouts and laughter of the escaping boy' have their parallel in her epiphanic recovery of her own past:

> She was conscious of a triumph over experience and earthly facts, a triumph magnificent, cold, hardly human, whose existence no one but herself would ever surmise. From the view-terrace she looked down on the perishing and perishable beauty of the valley, and, though she loved it no less, it seemed to be infinitely distant, like a valley in a star. At that moment, if kind voices had called her from the hotel, she would not have returned.   (p.307)

Like Eustace she is entirely true to her own vision. There is no breaking of faith, although it is worth noting the ironic echo in the name of the concierge, Feo, with its allusion to 'faith', but in a poetized or literary form that is appropriate to the false story in which he figured (the ordinary Italian word would have been *fede*).

Many of the early stories depend on a pattern involving a rupture between character and setting which is then generalized to individual and society. The details vary, but the pattern remains constant. All the characters, save the hero(ine), merge into a single and complicitous 'other': Colonel Leyland and Feo in 'The Eternal Moment', the narrator and Gennaro in 'The Story of a Panic', Inskip and Worters in 'Other Kingdom', the daughter and the tourists in 'The Road from Colonus'. Although the fictions derive much of their energy from their vivid realizing of a 'real world' in all its specificity and comic detailing, that world is nonetheless repudiated in the central character's solitary and transforming vision. (This is true even of 'The Road from Colonus', where, in the querulous aftermath of the failed vision, Mr Lucas is still granted a human presence allowed no other character.) The fantastic in Forster's writing is entirely in the service of that vision, functioning both as a strategy of concealment for the writer and, from the perspective of the central character, of revelation.

However, there is one form of the fantastic with which Forster experimented where he, at least superficially, followed the norms and conventions of what we now know as science fiction, or, as it was called at the turn of the century, 'scientific romance' or 'scientific fantasy'. But 'The Machine Stops' (1909), the often-anthologized evidence of this experiment, is at least as much a polemic against as an example of the genre whose practices and forms it so deftly uses.

Forster himself described it as 'a counterblast to one of the heavens of H. G. Wells' (*CT*, pp. vii–viii), referring, most likely, to such texts as 'A Story of the Days to Come' (1899), 'When the Sleeper Wakes' (1899), *Anticipations* (1901), *Mankind in the Making* (1902) and *A Modern Utopia* (1905). All of these depend in varying degree on the assumption of a technologically advanced future society. Even the somewhat more fancifully imagined *The Food of the Gods and How It Came to Earth* (1904) and *In the Days of the Comet* (1906) may have been the object of Forster's 'counterblast'. These last two were in fact described by Wells some years later as 'distinctly on the optimistic side'. Not that Wells's view of human nature was particularly Panglossian; he claimed to be 'neither a pessimist nor an optimist . . . [for] this is an entirely indifferent world in which wilful wisdom seems to have a perfectly fair chance'.[10] But for Wells, 'wilful wisdom' could properly be directed at inventing machines that would ease life's physical difficulties, thus transforming society and solacing the spirit. Such a meliorist point of view was, of course, totally antithetical to Forster's. In a diary entry of 1908 (the year in which he was writing 'The Machine Stops'), Forster makes this clear in terms that are particularly pertinent to this story: 'No more fighting, please, between the soul and the body, until they have beaten their common enemy, the machine' (16 June 1908, KCC).

Indeed, such a statement could well be regarded as the essayistic kernel of his fiction. For this story, like 'Mr Andrews' and 'The Other Side of the Hedge', develops its generating idea both fictionally and discursively. The idea both precedes and is embedded in the story, taking its fictional form in Kuno's defiance of the machine by his physical strength. Since it was then 'a demerit to be muscular' (*CT*, p. 166), his refusal to let his body become 'a swaddled lump of flesh' (p. 144) was in itself a moral act which had the practical consequence of allowing his escape. It is precisely because he resists the machine on a physical level, because he insists upon presence and touch, that he can fight the machine with his soul. Unlike the others, he is not 'seized with the terrors of direct experience' (p. 154); on the contrary, he seeks that experience, searching, like Dante's pilgrim, for a glimpse of the stars.

The metaphor for Kuno's quest – the constellation Orion – is, like Hermes as the spirit of fantasy, part of Forster's private myth-making. From *The Longest Journey* onward, Orion, in his frosty glories, rising in autumn with his promise of freedom, provided a nucleus of important associations and constituted a radiant image of desire. Within the story, the image has both personal significance for Kuno and a generalized relevance for those fragments of humanity who were waiting 'in the mist and the ferns until our civilization stops'. When the whole hideous edifice of 'our civilization' comes crashing down, the 'untainted sky' (*CT*, p. 197) and the stars remain, especially those stars that suggest a man: 'The four big stars are the man's shoulders and his knees. The three stars in the middle are like the belts that men wore once, and the three stars hanging are like a sword' (p. 147).

His attempts to make his mother understand this 'idea' fail, for she still believes that it is the machine that is the measure of all things, not man as Kuno has come to understand. But Kuno's insight, won even at the cost of his hideous maiming by the worm-like mending apparatus, that 'a man of my sort lived in the sky' (p. 179), is literally as well as metaphorically true. Even the landscape partakes of this anthropomorphic quality: 'to me they [the hills] were living and the turf that covered them was a skin, under which their muscles rippled' (p. 175).

It is Kuno's voice, especially in his account of his attempted escape, that is closest to the narrator's, but the narrative point of view stays with Vashti. The effect is, in a sense, to split the narrator's function, for he is both satirist and meditator. But, as the story moves to its climax, the satiric voice that in the first two sections parodied utopian language and, for a large part of the third, dystopian conventions, merges with the meditative in an apocalyptic vision of the end of things. Primarily, however, the narrator is an essayist, looking for a fictional analogue for a metaphysical speculation. Indeed, from the very first line, when he invites the reader to assist him in this search ('imagine, if you can . . .' – p. 144), it is clear that the fiction is subordinate to the discourse: 'It was thus that she opened her prison and escaped – escaped in the spirit: at least so it seems to me, ere my meditation closes. That she escapes in the body – I cannot perceive that' (p. 195). The narrator is both inside and outside the fiction; what he is looking at is an abstraction that temporarily has assumed human, i.e. fictional, form.

The story thus conflates a fictional and an essayistic perspective through a voice that would seem intrusive even in so highly determined a fiction as 'The Celestial Omnibus' but that here seems perfectly at home. For in 'The Machine Stops' the voice is the story; everything else is secondary to it. The conventions of 'scientific fantasy' function chiefly to give human scale to ideas, but these ideas are what the story is about. (This nicely reverses one of the points of satire within the fiction. In this future world everyone always talks of 'new ideas', but only if they are detached from direct experience. To Vashti, Kuno's 'idea that they [the stars in Orion] were like a man' [p. 147] is incomprehensible.) Thus, if in 'The Story of a Panic' closure was achieved in the telling but not the told, here the process is reversed. What is told is complete: 'The world, as they understood it, ended' (p. 192). But telling – here coextensive with a voice located on the boundary between essay and fiction, and speaking through those figures it has asked the reader to imagine – is not confined by fictional closure and is, indeed, the major creation of the text.

'The Machine Stops' focuses many of the issues raised in the first four chapters – story as essay, story as private myth, story as vehicle for voice. It further illustrates what may be called the salvation paradigm that Forster described in his *Commonplace Book*: 'Two people pulling each other into salvation is the only theme I find worthwhile' (p. 55). Certainly the movement from confusion to salvation is both organizing principle and primary thematic concern in nearly every story. Sometimes the line between the two poles – confusion and salvation – is straight, as in 'Mr Andrews' or 'The Celestial Omnibus'; sometimes curving, as in 'The Other Side of the Hedge', or even more indirect, as in 'The Machine Stops' when Vashti finally breaks her complicity with the others to take the hand of her son; and sometimes it is involuted and tortuous, as in 'The Life to Come' and 'The Other Boat'. Even in stories where it doesn't function, 'The Eternal Moment' or 'Arthur Snatchfold' for example, it offers an oblique comment on the ironically disclosed turn of events. Indeed the later story presents the exact reversal of the ending of the much earlier one. For in that story it is as if the Feo of 'The Eternal Moment' had become a worthy object. As the unheroic Sir Richard Conway is forced to confront his own diminished life, he knows that he is not saved in the terms that the salvation paradigm would suggest, although Arthur Snatchfold had certainly saved him in the more worldly terms Conway has based his life on.

Finally one may observe that 'Arthur Snatchfold' is not only an example of the story as novel in all its finely ironic social detailing, but, even more, like 'The Machine Stops', an example of the story as essay. Its great achievement is to endow Conway's moment of recognition with enormous human weight, making that moment comment on his entire life in the way such revelations do in Chekhov and Mansfield. Unlike Mansfield, however, who constructed such moments chiefly to illuminate her character (or to shock the reader into an equivalent illumination), Forster continues to speak through his character, never losing sight of the discursive argument that the character is made to bear, and bear the more impressively because of the human specificity with which he is invested. It is as if in 1928 Maurice (whose novel, of course, had not been published) had been growing older along with his now middle-aged creator and was being reconsidered from something of the perspective Forster would take many years later still, when in his terminal note to the final revision of that novel he would acidly conclude, 'Clive on the bench will continue to sentence Alec in the dock. Maurice may get off.'

5

The Historical Imagination

I THE RECOLLECTION OF THE PAST

In his 1929 essay on Proust, Forster described Marcel at the end of *A la recherche du temps perdu* in terms particularly applicable to his own writing: 'the hero starting out to be an author, rummaging in his past, disinterring forgotten facts, . . . that instant is the artist's instant; he must simultaneously recollect and create' (*AH*, p. 98). Forster was, indeed, an archaeologist of the human experience; all his writing, fiction and non-fiction alike, constitutes an exploration, a recovery, and finally the creation of the past. We have seen the beginning of this process at the very instant of Forster's 'starting out' – in the early essay 'Cnidus', and in many of the stories discussed in the preceding pages. But Forster's past is never entirely personal, never uniquely his alone. For, even when it is personal, it is public as well: a collective past explored by way of constituting an individual present.

The most intricate example of this manner of recovering the past is *Pharos and Pharillon*, Forster's Paterian memoir of his three years in Alexandria during the First World War.[1] That city presented countless paradoxes to Forster's own paradoxical sensibility as he explored her past in the roles of tourist, Red Cross worker, lover, reader, historian, guide, novelist and friend. For, if her past was infinitely more interesting than her somewhat dull and prosperous present, Forster's personal present, under the influence of what he later described as 'the slow Levantine degringolade' ('The Lost Guide',[2] KCC), was an exciting, transforming moment in his life. His 'part[ing] with respectability',[3] his love for Mohammed el Adl, and his friendship with the poet Cavafy, made him feel particularly atuned to this 'civilization of eclecticism and exiles'.[4] Its variety and its withholding of judgement were the most important of its qualities: 'The city symbolizes for me a mixture, a bastardy, an idea which I find congenial and opposed to that sterile idea of 100% in something or other that has impressed the modern world and forms the backbone of its blustering nationalisms' ('The Lost Guide',

KCC). Although these words were written after the Second World War, they express a sensibility clearly formed by the First, in particular by the experience of Alexandria. Moreover, Alexandria was the city of romance, of the love of Alexander for Hephaestion and of the love between Antony and Cleopatra. And, while 'nothing of the Alexandria they knew survives, except sea, sand and little birds',[5] the twitter of those birds at a modern concert could bridge the millennia for Forster, opening an access to the past by which he could both create and interpret his present.

Pharos and Pharillon is a generic hybrid, in part journalism, historical sketch, short story and essay. In its chapters, Forster assumes the identity of the ancient lighthouse (he signed himself 'Pharos' in the *Egyptian Mail*, where many of these pieces first appeared) to illuminate the city's past. The Alexandria of his experience, the Alexandria of his intellectual inquiry and the Alexandria of his imagination fuse first in the portrait of a city understood through her history, then in the portrait of the poet Cavafy, who epitomizes both the city's past and its present, and whose poetry is itself in large measure a meditation on history. Just out of focus, but still a felt presence, is the writer, like his hero, Cavafy, 'motionless at a slight angle to the universe' (*PP*, p. 91).

Cavafy's importance for Forster's development, especially for *A Passage to India*, has been several times examined. The fullest discussion, by Jane Lagoudis Pinchin, is notable for the serious attention it gives to *Pharos and Pharillon* (more often than not the book either is ignored or is acknowledged as an agreeable trifle, appropriate perhaps to its time and place but not to be taken too seriously). Reading Forster's essays through a detailed knowledge of Cavafy's poetry, she shows how both writers developed an ironic vision that they situated in the space between their subjects' experiences and their own – 'A moment in time and space. History as fiction.'[6] It is this observation that I want to examine here but with a somewhat different emphasis from Pinchin's, reading *Pharos and Pharillon* as a memoir, not so much of events but of the spirit. In another essay on Proust, Forster spoke of how Proust 'found in memory the means of interpreting and humanizing this chaotic world' (*TC*, p. 219). Forster did as well, although his memories refer less to the self than to human experience in a generalized sense. There is an impersonal quality to them; they are best negotiated through others – Goldsworthy Lowes Dickinson, Marianne

Thornton or, here, the vastly heroic Alexander, the enigmatic but powerful Cavafy.

Nonetheless, behind this clearly public text, this 'book about Alexandria' as an early dust jacket described it, there is private recollection. Behind the historian's reconstructions of the past, a figure beckons, at once mythical and real. He is Hermes, first met in the dedication as 'Hermes Psychopompos', conductor of souls, and again in the concluding pageant, where we see him in that role leading the shades to the asphodel. Hermes, however, has another name, that of Forster's dead friend Mohammed el Adl, the entire text an offering to his memory, indeed the result of his memory: 'I have written a story because of you and dedicated a book to you' ('The Letter-Book to Mohammed el Adl', KCC[7]). The story, as we saw in Chapter 3, was 'The Life to Come', the outlet for his 'indignation'; the book was *Pharos and Pharillon*, its dedication 'two words in Greek that fit book and him extraordinarily well' (letter to Florence Barger, 7 July 1922, KCC). In it the presence of Hermes–Mohammed frames Forster's descent into the past and re-emergence into his own present. It is a spiritual voyage taken under the guidance of one who, by making half of that journey, enabled Forster to complete the return.

Although the chapters were written separately, they cohere remarkably well. This is due in part to the integrity and accuracy of Forster's imagination of history, his ability to evoke, interpret and spiritually repossess those moments 'in space and time' on which his lighthouse beam casts momentary illumination. It is also due to the power of the metaphors established in the book's dedication, introduction and retrospective close. Particularly important are images of sequence – time as measured by the subsiding of the sea, by the forming of the Nile delta – that develop into images of cycle, of yearly repetition, what Forster described as 'the quiet persistence of the earth'. There is process and the arresting of process. 'Everything passes', he states at the close, and then the qualification that allows for his own witness, 'or almost everything' (*PP*, p. 98). It is a perspective, furthermore, that has a particularly Paterian resonance as it recalls Marius's sense of change and loss balanced by what Pater calls 'subjective immortality'.[8]

It is in that space that the pageant of *Pharos and Pharillon* (its form is essentially processional) unfolds. There is first the history of the lighthouse, one of the ancient wonders of the world, and of those lesser structures that followed, one of which was Pharillon, until it

'slid unobserved into the Mediterranean' (p. 10). Then follows a set
of historical portraits: a world conqueror, several Church fathers, a
few emperors and a poem. The poem is Cavafy's 'The God
Abandons Antony', and by its tone of stoic elegy (for by then the
god had abandoned the city) it links the two sections. It is
appropriate both to those distant shades that make their brief
appearance in 'Pharos', and to the modern city depicted in
'Pharillon', which, unlike its predecessors, 'calls for no enthusiastic
comment' (p. 98). Indeed the modern city is very lightly sketched.
Approached through an eighteenth-century account, it is seen in
two quick vignettes, whose somewhat desultory quality, amusing
but inconsequential, bears out that lack of enthusiasm. Only the city
as a palimpsest of maps, of streets whose names recall other names
and whose present dull gentility can be dismissed by a willed vision
of its 'vanished glory' excites the imagination. One curious feature
of the composition of this section is that, whereas Forster used all
the published historical essays for 'Pharos', he severely limited the
contemporary sketches for 'Pharillon'. Moreover, among the pieces
omitted were three of the best (all on music), whose inclusion would
have disturbed the design – that is, would have upset the
equilibrium – of the final text.

For it is the city of the past that Forster is intent on recovering. His
own itineraries are important chiefly as they trace the footsteps of
those past inhabitants whose portraits he is drawing. Like
Theocritus, whose poetry he characterizes in his other Alexandrian
book, *Alexandria: A History and a Guide*, Forster 'evoked an entire city
from the dead and filled its streets with men'.[9] His is a form of
history-writing akin to poetry; indeed, as has been frequently
argued, any attempt to fuse 'events, whether imaginary or real, into
a comprehensible totality . . . is a poetic process'.[10] And this is
strikingly so in Forster's case, for whom the instinct for pattern and
for the metaphor which is at once tenor and vehicle is manifest in a
language notable for its density of affect and allusion. Forster's was
an essayistic time. Everyone talked prose, although unlike
Monsieur Jourdain they may have been surprised to discover they
weren't talking poetry. Forster was one who most nearly did.

Of course, fiction is what is meant as the inclusive category in the
reference to the poetic process; that is, the historian by the very act
of ordering his materials creates something that never existed
before. Paradoxically, the more complete this fictional process, the
greater becomes its claim to a prior reality. What gives this fictive

reality to Forster's writing in *Pharos and Pharillon*, however, is not simply a novelist's trick of making real, of creating the illusion of a singular occurrence, but has to do with the fundamental relationship of Forster to his materials. For Forster the study of history was an act of self-scrutiny. He encountered his subjects as intimates, testing the degree to which he and they were like or unlike, entering their controversies to find the human link between himself and them. This is an attitude toward the past traceable to his earliest historical writing – the essay on Gemistus Pletho, for example. However, there the barrier of Pletho's personality tensed the encounter, although the link of spiritual sympathy was still the starting point. And that link remains the starting point in nearly all his later excursions into history. Even as late as 1942, in an entry in his *Commonplace Book*, he read the past in these terms. There he transcribed passages from Augustine, Pelagius, Jerome, looking for causes for the fall of Rome within the context of the possible fall of Europe, wondering in particular if there were a '*connection* between anti-sex and the Fall of Rome' (p. 133). He read in his sources, approving or questioning, admonishing or sympathizing, but always returning to the personal: 'Pelagius = Morgan, I am glad to say' (p. 134; he sympathized with the errors for which his 'namesake' – he was probably referring to the fact that both 'Pelagius' and 'Morgan' can be traced back to a word meaning 'sea' – was condemned at Carthage); or, a few pages later, 'Now farewell St Jerome for ever, but I must not ignore some similarities between us . . .' (p. 137). It is a point of view in which history is always other and self. Identifying this double focus is essential to understanding the role Forster cast for himself as Alexandria's historian.

Such a point of view is nowhere more clearly visible than in 'The Return from Siwa', the account of the city's 'founder' at that moment when 'his aspirations alter', when he ceases to 'regard Greece as the centre of the world'. Forster was always moved by the heroic follower of instinct even as he was well aware of the dangers: Alexander had 'caught, by the unintellectual way, a glimpse of something great, if dangerous'. The danger is believing oneself divine, the 'impartial ruler beneath whom harmony shall proceed', for, as Forster warns, 'that way lies madness'. But he was attracted all the same: 'to us, who cannot have the perilous honour of his acquaintance, he grows more lovable now than before', i.e. now when his aspirations are global and not merely a 'narrow little antiquarian crusade'. This combination of attraction and uneasiness is conveyed as well by the rhetorical mode Forster uses, irony tempered with vision and prophecy. Even though the actual encounter between priest and conqueror at the oasis is sketched from an ironic perspective (the critical moment turning on a grammatical error: the priest had 'meant to say Paidion ("my child") and said Paidios ("O Son of God") instead'), almost debunking the event, especially through the allusion to Walter Savage Landor's comically imagined conversation, Forster still invests it with a troubling mystery: 'The priest of Amen had addressed him as "Son of God". What exactly did the compliment mean? Was it explicable this side of the grave?' (*PP*, pp. 26–7).

What was it like to be Alexander, to have kingdoms at your feet? The essay neither asks such questions directly, nor provides answers. But it does open an interior access to such speculation, not through the devices of the historical novelist – breakfast in ancient Siwa, dinner in Athens – but through the imagination of a moralist bent on discovering the origins of a kind of human consciousness. The scenes it imagines are both singular and exemplary and they participate in a time scheme that is at once epic and local. The singular act, riding 'with a few friends into the western desert' (p. 24), occurs in a sentence in which the nations Alexander conquered pile up in the subordinate clause. The landscape Forster paints to accompany the ride, a landscape that has withstood the millennia and is thus his as much as it was Alexander's, is also within this dual focus: it was once, it has always been – 'Around him little flat pebbles shimmered and danced in the heat, gazelles stared, and pieces of sky slopped [*sic*] into the sand' (p. 25).

There is no facile equating of the writer's experiences with those of his subject, but there is the successful effort of imagination that allows him to speak his concerns through another. The most moving moment in the essay from this point of view occurs in the scene of Alexander's death. It is described in the form of a question in which the dominant metaphor of military conquest is sustained but turned around. Who conquered whom? The question is left open: 'When at the age of thirty-three he died, when the expedition that he did not seek stole towards him in the summer-house at Babylon, did it seem to him as after all but the crown of his smaller quests?' (p. 27).

The concern with death is never far from the surface of Forster's writing, and was, indeed, specifically tied up with the question of writing itself. In a letter to Goldsworthy Lowes Dickinson written just as he was completing *Pharos and Pharillon* he makes the connection explicit:

> I am bored not only by my creative impotence, but by the tiresomeness and conventionalities of fiction-form: e.g. the convention that one must view the action through the mind of one of the characters; and say of the others 'perhaps they thought', or at all events adopt their view-point for a moment only. If you can pretend you can get inside one character, why not pretend it about all the characters? I see why. The illusion of life may vanish, and the creator degenerate into the showman. Yet some change of the sort must be made[.] The studied ignorance of novelists grows wearisome. They must drop it. Also they must recapture their interest in death, not that they ever had it much, but the Middle Ages had it, and the time for re[-]examination is overdue.
>
> (8 May 1922, L&F, II, 26)

Alexander's death, like Harold's in 'The Point of It', becomes for Forster a focus for his own meditations. Recovering that moment becomes part of the process of finding his way anew in his own writing, particularly in *A Passage to India*. Furthermore, the form that the meditation takes, the historical essay in which private concerns are transmuted into public ones, will indeed remain his dominant mode.[11] Thus, both in formal and thematic terms, *Pharos and Pharillon* stands in relation to all his subsequent writing as the crucial linking text.

The main preoccupation, however, in the 'Pharos' chapters concerns theology rather than heroism and conquest. For the most part Forster's stance is one of detachment, although he does take sides. Arius is much to be preferred over St Athanasius, a remarkable politician and one who knew how to inspire enthusiasm but of whom 'not one single generous action . . . is recorded' (*PP*, p. 49). Even so, Forster had little of Gibbon's animus toward the early Church, rather a bemused sadness that so much was lost as a result of these endless controversies. In much the same way that he could understand Alexander's dreams of conquest, he could understand how future emperors could be 'drawn into the dance of theology, none more so than Julian, who dreamed of Olympus' (p. 50). It is the controversy over Arianism that elicits that remark and here Forster is no mere observer, for to the degree that he was a Christian he was an Arian. It was, after all, a position that brought Christ closer to man, 'indeed, to level him into a mere good man. . . . This appealed to the untheologically-minded – to Emperors, and particularly to Empresses. It made them feel less lonely' (p. 50). Forster's view here is barely distinguishable from Kuno's in 'The Machine Stops' as he imagines a Christ–Orion, the 'man of my sort [who] lived in the sky' (*CT*, p. 179).

He joins this controversy precisely because he values the human tendency to 'substitute the human for the divine', suspecting 'that many an individual Christian to-day is an Arian without knowing it' (*PP*, p. 51). What he valued in the early Church were 'her traditions of scholarship and tolerance' (p. 50), particularly as they were personified in Clement of Alexandria before 'Christianity . . . descended with a double-edged sword that hacked the ancient world to pieces' (p. 42). Indeed it is Clement even more than Arius who personifies the city. He came earlier, before the controversies had grown rigid; he would mock rather than denounce his opponents, for he lived in a city where 'conciliation must have seemed more possible than elsewhere, and the graciousness of Greece not quite incompatible with the Grace of God' (p. 42). But, *inter alia*, *Pharos and Pharillon* is an elegy to just that incompatibility.

The last of the theological controversies that Forster details with a remarkable accuracy and a vividness not usually found in such expositions, concerns the monophysite heresy, 'Timothy the Cat and Timothy Whitebonnet'. In a playful but not really facetious fashion (this despite his own comments in a letter to Trevelyan [16 Nov 1917, KCC], and the view of most critics, particularly those following Trilling), he outlines the positions, making it clear that the line between heresy and orthodoxy is quite accidental. It was a controversy that could have been resolved one way; it just happened to have been resolved in another. That discussion closes with a remark that, while ending both chapter and section, opens the text to quite different considerations from those involved in this particular dispute: 'The Pharos, the Temple of Serapis – these have perished, being only stones, and sharing the impermanence of material things. It is ideas that live' (*PP*, p. 55). But what ideas? Does one include the hair-splittings that distinguish a Timothy the Cat from a Timothy Whitebonnet? Within the context of the chapter, the answer must be yes. Yet if such a sentence as 'It is ideas that live' is almost invariably spoken in a voice of self-congratulation, it is not so spoken here. For it is typical of Forster's complex voice that, while he can make such a statement, he is able at the same time to undermine its pretensions. He suggests that if it be true – and, yes, he thinks it is – it may be the cause of much more harm than good. The dominant note, however, is elegiac. The Pharos has fallen and that is what we hear echoed in the poem of Cavafy, 'The God Abandons Antony', that Forster prints as the bridge between the Alexandria of history and the Alexandria of his own experience.

However, he enters upon that present obliquely, the first chapter of 'Pharillon', 'Eliza in Egypt', describing the travels of an eighteenth-century lady possessed of a spiteful eye and a fang-like pen. She is a fitting emblem for the diminished world of 'Pharillon', just as Alexander was of the vaster world of 'Pharos'. Unlike Alexander, though, she completed her journey across India, where Forster leaves her, fixed in a photograph, 'attended in the background by a maid-servant and mosque' (p. 72). Alexander, on the other hand, world conquest unfinished, was left questioning the universe in the summer-house in Babylon. Eliza is nonetheless an unusual lens for Forster, who ordinarily works through a sensibility more akin to his own. He handles her much as he did St Athanasius, as one who reflects back the conditions he wishes to depict.

Except for the Eliza chapter, however, Forster is the central presence in the 'Pharillon' essays. Taken together they constitute a set of ironic footnotes to the sweep of history in 'Pharos': Eliza scaled down from Alexander; a comic visit to a hashish den where there was disappointingly little evidence of the drug (concluding with the statement, 'I could hardly help being sorry for poor sin' [p. 81], this in the city that had heard the thunders of the fathers of the Church). The essays touch on a few characteristic activities – the cotton exchange, cotton manufacture, the hashish den. They describe some streets and landscapes, but they clearly suggest that the glories of the past have vanished. Even the asphodel that grows in the Mariout country early in March is a coarse, harsh plant, a disappointment to those 'who dreamt of the Elysian Fields . . . too heavy for the hands of ghosts, too harsh for their feet' (p. 88).

The present, the 'Pharillon' essays suggest, is too solid, uninteresting. Except . . ., and suddenly Cavafy looms over the scene, the elegant, infinitely civilized poet of Alexandria's past and present. As Forster evokes his voice, we realize how familiar it has already become to us. Cavafy's conversation, for example, ranged rapidly from the 'tricky behaviour' of an emperor in 1096, to olives, friends, George Eliot, dialects and language (p. 92). The list of subjects reads like the table of contents to *Pharos and Pharillon* itself. Indeed it is 'Cavafian', rather than the more frequently used term

'Stracheyesque', that describes Forster's writing in this text. Cavafy, to be sure, was less of an historian, more of an elegist than Forster (as Strachey was the reverse). It was his special skill (as it was Forster's) that he could 'convey the obscurity, the poignancy, that sometimes arise together out of the past, entwined into a single ghost' (p. 96). Nonetheless his eroticized readings of the past were clearly like those Forster had already experimented with in 'The Tomb of Pletone' and 'Macolnia Shops'. Both in his choice of subject matter and in the way he modulated voice and stance, Cavafy offered Forster a revised and probably more durable form of Hellenism than the nostalgic, idealized Hellenism of *The Longest Journey* and *Maurice*[12] (more durable because, as in Donne's words, it could 'endure vicissitude, and season, like the grass').

But Cavafy's friendship was as important for Forster as was his writing. It seems both to have begun the freeing of his creative imagination and to have helped awaken his physical self. By the example of his own homosexuality, Cavafy apparently helped Forster to relax his guarded nature. Indeed, he helped him to act as Forster had himself recommended in a 1911 essay, 'The Beauty of Life': 'Why don't we trust ourselves more and the conventions less? . . . is it likely that life will give herself away to us, unless we also give ourselves away?' Some years later, in a paper for the Memoir Club, he obliquely (his favourite word for Cavafy, as it is most readers' for Forster) recalled that importance: 'Cavafy is never embittered, never the invalid [the point of comparison is Proust]. He is thankful to have lived and in that way – *and to me in other ways* – he is an example' (KCC).

Thus encouraged by Cavafy (and also by Edward Carpenter – Forster was in correspondence with Carpenter throughout this period and read his autobiography, *My Days and Dreams: Being Autobiographical Notes* [1916], with care and enthusiasm[13]), Forster translated Whitmanic metaphor into Whitmanic action. As a hospital-searcher for the Red Cross, he was, like Whitman a half-century earlier, in constant attendance on death. It is in these terms that he joins Mohammed in the figure of Hermes. But another mythic figure opens and closes the book as well: he is Menelaus, leader of the solid cotton-brokers in the concluding pageant. He opens the book somewhat inauspiciously ('The career of Menelaus was a series of small mishaps' – *PP*, p. 13) and closes it on the same note. Even so, Menelaus, bureaucrat, official, a member of the best society, is, as much as Hermes, a figure for the writer, for Forster, too, was bureaucrat (in a small way), official, and member of that society. And it is from this double perspective that he surveys the past, not only turning history into fiction, but also turning fiction into history, for many of his totally imaginary accounts, one feels, must have happened precisely as he describes them.

But the past constantly escapes, and, the more we fix it in words, the more it escapes irrevocably into fiction.[14] This is as true for the chronicling of the largest public events as it is for the recalling of the most private. As Forster wrote in the letter-book for Mohammed, some months after the news of his death had reached him, 'I write for my own comfort and to recall the past.' But, try as he might 'to keep this real, my own words get in the way' (KCC). The 'letter' is a record both of his memories and of the act of remembering, but it is also, most poignantly, a record of the betrayal of memory through writing. It is this collision of a reality, which is itself never constant, with the words that at once render it fiction that characterizes nearly all Forster's work in the historical mode.

The 'letter' also provides an interesting gloss on another Forster text, a gloss and possibly an inspiration. Forster wrote off and on in it from 5 August 1922 to 27 December 1929; less than two years later, in 1931, the Hogarth Press published in pamphlet form the text that later was republished in *Two Cheers for Democracy*, 'A Letter to Madan Blanchard'. Essay, memoir, history, conversation, short story, letter,[15] it stages an encounter that is purely imaginary but that at the same time distils the accumulated memories and longings of that other letter-book. That he chose the letter form for this 'essay' seems to me directly related to his seven-year long imaginary conversation with Mohammed. Furthermore, the 'characters' in it, Blanchard and Prince Lee Boo, can be read as variations on the writer and recipient of the letter that marked Mohammed's death at Mansourah.

Forster begins as an historian, reading in the London Library of an unlettered eighteenth-century sailor, a figure in the memoirs of a Captain Henry Wilson, who remained in the Pelew Islands when Wilson and the rest of the crew of the shipwrecked *Antelope* returned to England. Using the real memoirs of Captain Wilson, Forster creates a fictive encounter between his real self and that dimly perceived but, to Forster, psychologically real and immensely touching *alter ego*, the sailor who 'jibbed', who one day did the unexpected, who by going native seems to the twentieth-century writer to have been in possession of some wisdom, some truth, that he would dearly like to possess. The process of getting that truth is complexly ironic. As he writes in the London Library in 1931 to a recipient who cannot read, he must dissolve 150 years of real time. He runs it backwards, as he imagines his letter slowing down in its temporal regression – by air mail to Paris, but then, as it moves from Paris to Genoa to Egypt to India to Macao, it goes by ever slower overland routes and smaller ships until 'just one tiny ripple survives to float my envelope into your hand' (*TC*, p. 305).

Blanchard 'went native', and Forster wants to know why. 'I want to know why you stopped behind when the others went' (p. 306). Behind that question there are others: let me know how you are, have you gone off into darkness, or 'into what I can't help calling life' (p. 310)? There is the writer seated in the library, 'stuffed in between books, and old ladies with worried faces . . . making notes' (p. 306), but in his imagination cut loose from all civilizations and constraints, where books don't exist (and neither do ladies). And while he is in the one place he is also in the other. Reading of Blanchard he wonders why he is so set about by rules, why he can't keep his hat on in church, even when no one's looking, why he never manages to hit below the belt. It is precisely this sense of himself as one who never jibbed that gives such power to his conjuring of Blanchard out of the darkness of time. And that is why he studies history, he writes: to meet 'in the flesh' those who 'managed better' than he, 'the people who carried whimsicality into action, the salt of my earth . . . the solid fellows who suddenly jib' (p. 312).

However, this appropriating of another's history as his own produces a double text. For, if Blanchard went off into the darkness, Prince Lee Boo came back to England, back to light.

> The Company's plan was to educate him in England, and send him back to rule the islands for us; he was to take with him horses, dogs, cows, pigs, goats, seeds, clothes, rum, and all that makes life bearable; he was to oust Qui Bill from the succession, conquer the Artingalls with musket fire, and reign over corpses and coconuts in a gold-laced suit. (p. 307)

Of course this never happens, for Lee Boo is soon a corpse himself, dead at the age of twenty of the smallpox. Thus, if the primary text produces an encounter with the self, the sub-text yields an encounter with Mohammed (dead at the age of twenty-three of tuberculosis) in something of the same fashion as in 'The Life to Come'. This does not mean that Lee Boo or Vithobai in any sense equals Mohammed; indeed as human beings there is an enormous gulf between them. Mohammed was never seduced by Western civilization as the Prince was, nor was he vindictive (justifiably so, the story suggests) as Vithobai turned Barabbas became. Nonethless, Forster's bitterness against the destructive pretensions of empire is given fictional form in both story and essay. Lee Boo may have been too much of a 'puppet' to engage Forster's imagination fully – 'he was . . . too harmless . . . always did as he was bid, and people like that don't seem quite real' (p. 312) – but Forster could still use him as a potent emblem for that sense of indignation that Mohammed's death evoked, an indignation, however, that involved considerably more than the death of a single human being.

Forster used the essay–letter to explore a set of historic events within the context of private memory. His analysis yielded both a political and a psychological truth by means of a fictional representation. But it is by no means a reductive analysis; the tonal density of the writing assures that. He protected his subjects from sentimentality by turning his irony against his epistolary self (the hat in church, the gentleman writer amidst the ladies in the library). He allowed his own voice to sound, but he deflected it through his scholarly sources. Indeed, the footnotes and attributions are, to a degree, part of the fiction, for as much as he quotes he fabricates. The Madan Blanchard of history is, in fact, lost to history – 'what about your own relatives? I don't even know whether you're English or French' (p. 309). Thus it is the Blanchard of fiction who carries the Whitmanic affirmation of this historical meditation to its close (it is a meditation that merges Whitman and the Melville of *Typee* in opposition to a specifically Swiftian nihilism, especially in the references to the 'Irish clergyman' who 'invented a group of islands to relieve his feelings on' – *TC*, p. 313). That affirmative reply is itself part of the letter that discovers Blanchard in the first place. It is precisely the sort of reply that an unlettered sailor could produce as it is the only response that the many-lettered writer would want to receive. It contains a single word, a single letter, indeed a single sound signing its own meaning, ' "aaa" (Pelew for Yes)' (p. 314).

Both *Pharos and Pharillon* and 'A Letter to Madan Blanchard' are reflections of the same set of experiences. Each is narrated by an engaged historian whose researches were constantly being filtered through his own sensibility. Formally they are different sorts of texts, although each is a generic hybrid; yet they not only share a similar emotional core, but are empowered by a similar tension, given emblematic form in the figure of the man who jibbed. That figure is, after all, part of a recurring pattern in Forster's fiction from 'The Other Side of the Hedge' to 'The Other Boat'. In that early story, the speaker succeeds almost despite himself. In both *The Longest Journey* and *Where Angels Fear to Tread*, the pattern is used negatively, Rickie's tragic failure set in contrast to the essentially comic failure of Philip and Caroline. However, in *Maurice* the characters succeed, although one might argue that Forster does not follow through imaginatively in that decision. And in 'The Other Boat' Lionel is also granted a measure of success, although his is a perhaps more problematic, at least more Wagnerian, fate than Blanchard's. Even if that pattern is not part of the surface text of *Pharos and Pharillon* the dedication suggests that the text can be read as an elegy not only to Mohammed but also to the writer who did not jib, who did not do the unexpected, who, instead, returned to England to his writings and researches, but who found memory deceiving and the words that express it even more so.

II THE QUESTION OF STRACHEYISM

D. H. Lawrence's often-quoted response to *Pharos and Pharillon* raises the issue directly. 'Sad as ever,' he wrote to Forster in a 1924 letter, 'like a lost soul crying Ichabod. But I prefer the sadness to the Stracheyism' (quoted in Fur, II, 163). Although the remark probably reveals more about Lawrence than about Forster, it is worth examining in the context of a discussion of Forster's historical imagination. Lawrence seemed to require an incompetent Forster, someone who couldn't live in his own body, who, in Lawrence's somewhat absurd phrasing in an earlier letter to Bertrand Russell, refused to 'take a woman and fight clear to his own basic, primal being'.[16] Having created this version of his rival, he spent a good deal of time bemoaning its existence. One result was that he could only read Forster in terms of his construct, seeing in each work an illustration of a flawed and contradictory psyche. The opposition between 'sadness' and 'Stracheyism' identified for Lawrence what he elsewhere described as 'the feeling of acute misery [I get] from him', which he set in contrast to 'those clever little habits' which he felt Forster used to mask that misery.[17]

But does either term really apply? Although there is an undertone of personal sorrow in *Pharos and Pharillon*, it is transmuted into a generalized lament on the passing of all things. On the other hand, the text evokes such a pleasure in each of its moments, whether of the immediate present or of a thousand years past, that the elegiac impulse is often replaced by the celebratory. Forster clearly opened the possibility of a retrospective sadness, but, cannier than Lawrence gave him credit for being, he countered it with an ironic awareness of the self-indulgence such sadness involves. The essay 'The Consolations of History', written in the interval between his Alexandria experiences and the publication of *Pharos and Pharillon*, makes this point its primary thesis. The historian may, Forster suggests in his essay, forget his present powerlessness as he becomes a familiar of the powerful of the past, privy to their secrets, moving unimpeded through their private chambers. He thus may dally with the past, or censure it, or 'sweetest of all . . . pity [it] because [pity] subtly combines the pleasures of the other two', but that pity 'has nothing to do with sorrow, it has no connection with anything that one has personally known and held dear. It is half a sensuous delight, half gratified vanity.' History consoles because it temporarily imparts the illusion of immortality. ' "Dear dead woman with such hair too" ', murmurs the student, 'but not "I feel chilly and grown old." That comes with awakening' (*AH*, pp. 165–6).

Thus the sadness Lawrence claims to hear has, I am suggesting, little to do with Forster personally, although it may be an inevitable function of the way Forster views the past. He is not 'crying Ichabod' – that is, lamenting 'the glory that has departed from Israel' (see 1 Samuel 4:21, and for 'Israel' read 'Alexandria'), although he clearly thinks the modern city a dull descendant of the original. But it is only because Alexandria never really was glorious but was instead hospitable and open, a 'civilization of eclecticism and exile',[18] that he could feel so at his ease there. The sub-text, especially if we read it back through the letter-book to Mohammed, is a celebration rather than a lament.

That leaves the word 'Stracheyism', an epithet automatically accepted in most discussions of *Pharos and Pharillon* and of the historical essays. Wilfred Stone, for example, states that '*Pharos* shows Forster the historical biographer at the top of his form, working again in the manner of Lytton Strachey, as he had done earlier in such pieces as "Cnidus" (1905) and "Gemistus Pletho" (1905)'.[19] ('Cnidus' was, in fact, published in 1904 but largely written in 1903, as was 'Gemistus Pletho'). And in a footnote Stone describes the later essays on Gibbon and Voltaire as 'Strachey-like'. The only difficulty with this statement is that chronologically speaking it is Strachey who was 'Forster-like', certainly at the start, for 'Cardan', 'Gemistus Pletho' and 'Macolnia Shops' were all published *before* those essays of Strachey that could properly be labelled 'Stracheyesque'. Indeed, they were written before Strachey had published anything. Strachey's early essays for the *Spectator* are stylistically rather different from his later work, and only one was written before 1907, a neat but unexciting book review on the Empress Sophie and the Hanoverian Succession. His two other early biographical essays, written, as were Forster's, for the *Independent Review*, 'Mademoiselle Lespinasse' (1904) and 'Horace Walpole' (1904), are also book reviews and only show glimmers of the later manner. They are certainly not like the acts of historical imagination that Forster was performing in those same pages.

But the sense persists that the label may be right even if the chronology is wrong, especially in the later essays. The Gibbon and Voltaire essays make a good test case, for both Gibbon and Voltaire were immensely important for the intellectual development of Strachey and Forster; Voltaire in particular links the two twentieth-century writers. Strachey wrote three essays on Voltaire between 1914 and 1919 (and a fourth in 1931); indeed, as early as 1912 he contemplated writing a life of Voltaire, and to a certain degree saw himself as – or, at least as 'not yet [–] Voltaire'.[20] Forster saw him that way as well. In a radio broadcast several years after Strachey's death, Forster compared them:

> They both had intellectual integrity, were witty, fastidious, learned and mischievous, and believed in personal friendship. In one way, indeed, Voltaire was Strachey's superior; he has a burning passion for justice and would risk his life and position in order to rescue the innocent and the downtrodden. In another way Voltaire was inferior, for he wasn't a poet, although he wrote poetry, whereas Strachey, though he didn't write poetry, was a poet.   (3 Oct 1943, typescript, KCC)

Even more to the point is Forster's assessment of his own

relationship to Voltaire, for it identifies, too, an important difference between Strachey and himself. He had just transcribed into his *Commonplace Book* a passage from Voltaire's *Charles XII* describing the execution of Patkul, the French-born Russian ambassador to Charles's court.

> Each time I read the magnificent paragraph above – at last transcribed – I am struck by the economy of the *irony* and even of the *pathos*. Yet the whole passage vibrates with both[.] There is a sort of religious grandeur – cruelty and cowardice are both noted without contempt.
>
> When will there be such writing again . . . ? Voltaire and I do speak the same language, vast though be the difference in our vocabularies, we are both civilised. . . . We belong to the cultured interlude which came between the fall of barbarism and the rise of universal 'education'. We understand, for instance, that a good prose style doesn't hurry to make its point straight away, and that it's difficult to say where it does make its point. We believe in reason, in pity, and in not always coming out right – that is to say I hope to be logical and compassionate (V. thought he always could be), and I know that Patkul's wheel [the instrument of the ambassador's execution] may be waiting for me too.   (*CB*, pp. 97–8)

It is the juncture of irony and pathos that Forster finds so striking in Voltaire which most distinguishes him from Strachey. For Forster's ironic vision is founded on pathos (the quality Lawrence called 'sadness'?), a tonality and a perspective totally lacking in Strachey. It is to be sure a dangerous quality, so close is it to the sentimental. It rarely became that in Forster's writing, however, chiefly because his 'fear . . . for the collapse of Civilization' grounded all that he wrote from 1915 onward.[21] With Strachey, by contrast, irony covers all. It is globally non-discriminating even if it makes multiple distinctions in its local effects. Strachey stands at a far greater distance from his material than Forster does; his stance is essentially that of a collector or connoisseur, a constructor of cabinets of curiosity. To be sure, moral indignation and moral sympathy are often at work, but they rarely interfere with the elegant arrangement of details, the careful rotation of the subject so that different lights can play upon it, the telling juxtaposition, the artful tension between the unique and the exemplary.

In Strachey's essay 'A Sidelight on Frederick the Great', a review of *The Memoirs of Henri de Catt*, he uses a phrase that exactly describes his own perspective as a writer of history: 'the interest of the book is entirely personal and psychological. . . . The historian neglects Oliver Cromwell's warts; but it is just such queer details of physiognomy that the amateur of human nature delights in.'[22] As an 'amateur of human nature', Strachey enjoyed his subjects, rarely allowing the ridiculous to demean – indeed, using it to enhance the human actuality (Gibbon, for example is seen 'now almost spherical, bowl[ing] along the Bath Road in the highest state of exhilaration'[23]). However, as deeply sympathetic as Strachey was to Gibbon's enterprise, and as alive to its importance as 'one of the supreme monuments of Classic Art in European literature',[24] and as atuned as well to 'the irony beneath the pomp' of his prose, he nonetheless kept his subject at a safe distance: 'At every period of his life [Gibbon was] . . . a pleasant thing to contemplate'.[25] The chief emotion that Strachey communicates is a satisfaction with his own arrangement of his materials. One is always conscious of an effect being aimed at, and, more often than not, an effect being achieved.

The contrast between Forster's and Strachey's Gibbon essays is illuminating. The first of Forster's two essays, 'Captain Edward Gibbon' (1931), follows Strachey's by three years. In some ways it is a narrower undertaking, in so far as it focuses on Gibbon's three years in the Hampshire Militia and is not an epitome of his entire career. At several points, however, it sounds a good deal like Strachey's; some sentences could almost appear in one as readily as in the other. First Strachey:

> He drove a straight, firm road through the vast unexplored forest of Roman history; his readers could follow with easy pleasure along the wonderful way; they might glance, as far as their eyes could reach, into the entangled recesses on either side of them; but they were not invited to stop, or wander, or camp out, or make friends with the natives; they must be content to look and pass on.[26]

Now Forster:

> Thus the lane that passes under this garden reminds me at moments of the enormous stretches of road he was later to

traverse – the roads that led all over Europe and back through the centuries into Rome, then all over Europe again until they frayed out in the forests of Germany and the sands of Syria.   (*AH*, p. 218)

This thinking through metaphor, following the logic of the image to its conclusion so that figuration is more substantive than decorative, is a trait of Bloomsbury writing, as P. N. Furbank has shown.[27] But there are important differences. To begin with, the sentences perform different functions in their respective essays. Strachey's is concerned with Gibbon's control of his audience; it identifies the writer–reader relationship. Forster's moves from his relationship with his subject to his subject's relationship to his material. It is also much less formally plotted. Strachey's proliferating independent clauses, neatly joined by semi-colons, create a cartographical effect; clause joins to clause as road to road. It elegantly mimes its generating metaphor and in its control of its audience it enacts its central point as well. With Forster the metaphor is not so much employed as tested. There is no assurance when the sentence begins as to how it will turn out. But the writing, far from being shapeless, has an enveloping rhythm and pattern of alliteration and repetition that make it closer to poetry than to prose.

Forster is also a much nearer presence than Strachey. As the opening of the essay makes clear, Gibbon's road is in some literal sense his own:

The garden where I am writing slopes down to a field, the field to a road, and along that road exactly a hundred and seventy years ago passed a young officer with a rather large head. If he had turned the head to the right, he would have seen not me, not the garden, but he would have seen the elms that still border the garden – they were already recognizable trees.   (p. 212)

In much the same way as Forster's visit to the Mariout country outside Alexandria revealed to him just such a sloping sky and staring gazelles as Alexander must have seen, so his own visit to Hampshire, both literally and metaphorically, opens out on the road that Gibbon travelled. Embedded in the happy coincidence is a small detail that becomes, from the retrospect of Forster's present situation, immensely moving – the trees are the same. Thus here, as in so many of the essays, a place is made for Forster's own witness.

His essays are extrapolations of a mind engaged in its explorations.

Even the similarities of authorial voice between Strachey and Forster are more apparent than real. The colloquial, the conversational and the ironic are traits of both, but Strachey's was a far more polished style, more epigrammatic and constructed around antitheses and parallels, than was Forster's. He rarely used the first person, the generalized 'one' functioning in its place. Forster, by contrast, is a constant presence: his mind at work on his materials is the primary activity of each essay, a speaking 'I', the dominating focus. Gibbon's own style was, of course, almost totally epigrammatic, a result of his aim 'to achieve a sententious and oracular brevity'.[28] However, Gibbon's 'we' did not speak for his readers but directly and personally to them. Leo Braudy's comment on Gibbon's presence in his text seems to me to apply with equal aptness to Forster as well: 'The final impression the reader keeps of the *Decline and Fall* is of the mind which created it.'[29] It is in this sense that Forster, although working in a very different stylistic mode, is more nearly in touch with Gibbon's achievement than Strachey, despite Strachey's and Gibbon's shared epigrammatic manner.

Forster, of course, was an historical essayist not an historian, but despite the great difference in scale between their projects (a difference he would have been the first to insist on), Forster's reading of Gibbon exerted a continual pressure on his own writing. Thus the emphasis in this discussion is twofold, for I wish to show both how Forster's reading of Gibbon helps explain his own historical project and how Forster's essays on Gibbon are its best illustration. The statement that makes this connection most clearly occurs in the 1941 broadcast reprinted as an essay in *Two Cheers for Democracy*, 'Gibbon and his *Autobiography*', where he describes Gibbon as 'a man of letters, equipped for evoking and interpreting the past' (*TC*, p. 159). The doublet is particularly important for Forster, for whom the writing of history was primarily an act of evocation. To achieve this, Forster used the techniques of the novelist far more than Gibbon did, but the resulting vivid intimacy and the sense of multiple and contingent explanations for any occurrence that underlies his historical analysis have their parallel in Gibbon's procedures.[30]

If Forster the essayist operated with the visual imagination of the novelist, it was a visual imagination of a highly self-reflexive nature. Typically he creates a scene, often discovered in his reading, but drawn with his own emphases and purposes, and then he proceeds to scrutinize it, playing the exegete in something of the same manner he developed for the 'reading' of the vase in the Kirchner Museum in 'Macolnia Shops'. Forster finds a mention in Gibbon's journal of a visit to Dorking, 'a whimsical pretty place in the style of Vauxhall' (*AH*, p. 212), and then examines guidebooks of the period until he is able to reconstruct one of the whimsicalities, a depiction of the Valley of the Shadow of Death, where the Libertine is pictured dying, surrounded by his corrupting books, his Tindal and his Hobbes. 'The young officer must have regarded the alcove with an easy and an equal smile', foreseeing that 'before long, in the Libertine's library, a work of his own would be lying, . . . *The Decline and Fall of the Roman Empire*' (p. 213). The moment in Dorking is largely Forster's creation. He uses it as a *tableau vivant* to introduce Gibbon into the essay (his name has not yet been mentioned), connecting it with the opening scene of the writer in the garden looking down the road Gibbon had travelled exactly 170 years earlier, and using both scenes as means to explore the figure now coming into focus from his journal. The exploratory quality of Forster's essay is enhanced by his use of an exploratory text as his primary material. For it is not *The Decline and Fall* nor even the *Autobiography* but Gibbon's private journals (unlike the various versions of the *Memoirs*, these were *not* intended for publication; the *Memoirs* were commonly called the *Autobiography* and were so called in the edition Forster used) that he bases his essay on. And, unlike the later figure, when Gibbon 'was worried and when he was young, he did not always know what he wanted to say' (*AH*, p. 215).

The question that constitutes the sub-text is: what are the sources of the historian's power? The anecdotal form of that question is: how did his years in the Hampshire Militia help the future historian of Rome? The Hampshire lane becomes, metaphorically, the road that will lead all over Europe and back through the centuries to Rome. But this road is not merely a road into books. It is the means by which the historian may gain 'some conception of how men who are not historians behave', for 'otherwise he will move in a world of the dead' (p. 218). Historians must have knowledge, and Gibbon had genius to boot, but what particularly moves Forster in this early journal are those qualities that connect Gibbon with the generality of mankind rather than those (by far the more obvious ones) that set him apart. Thus the present historian keeps his eye on the past historian, 'the greatest [that] England has ever produced' (pp.

213–14), until he rides out of view. He is conscious of the 'romance' of his literary effort, conscious as well that Gibbon found no romance in the tiresome circumstances of his militia service. But he uses the absence of romance both to characterize his own point of view and to set off the striking contrast between Gibbon's early literary projects and the one that a few years later 'started to . . . mind' when 'musing amidst the ruins of the Capitol' he heard 'vespers in the Temple of Jupiter' in what is now the Church of the Ara Coeli.[31]

The details of the essay are very intricately woven. There is time in its very few pages to catch quickly a few moments of a vanished past: methods of conscription for the Seven Years War, the bill of fare for a dinner for the Burgesses of Southampton, gossip from the funeral of George II, the petty squabbles between the commanders of the North Hampshire and South Hampshire militias 'engaged in a war otherwise unknown to history' (*AH*, p. 213). But the casual, anecdotal manner is deceiving. No details are superfluous; all are drawn into the central meditation and give it density. If from the retrospect of the close the essay seems carefully plotted, moving from particular to generalization to closure, at the start the possibilities are multiple. A moment is conjured up, a question is posed and a quest is undertaken so that each conclusion is newly won. There are no answers laid out beforehand. Strachey, by contrast, is a presenter. One feels his Gibbon to have existed entire before one word of the essay was written. There is very little of the quality of trial, the emphasis falling rather on finish. In this sense Strachey is Bronzino to Forster's Titian, a comparison that implies no disparagement but does identify an important difference.

A similar strategy of calling up a scene, posing a question and considering possible responses structures the two Voltaire essays, printed together in *Abinger Harvest* under the title 'Voltaire's Laboratory'. Here the subject is Voltaire the scientist; he is seen first in an iron foundry weighing molten metal, then in his charming apartment in Cirey, the house of Madame de Chatelet, surrounded by his clocks and scales, his thermometers, barometers, pans, crucibles and retorts. And in her apartment Madame de Chatelet is similarly in view, scorching vegetables, weighing the results, writing up the experiments 'far into the night . . . and between them slumbers the dilapidated central portion of the house, possibly occupied by her husband' (p. 201). But, as skilled as he was in evoking the amusing and the incongruous, Forster is only incidentally interested in such aspects of his subject. His aim is rather to explore a mentality, a way of thinking, or, more precisely, an attitude toward knowledge.

Thus the essays implicitly pose a twofold question: what did Voltaire think he was engaged in as he weighed his metals, decapitated his snails and slugs, poured vinegar on Mont Blanc; and what in fact was he engaged in? Forster does not need to establish Voltaire's seriousness or even competence as a scientist (in this sense the essay is quite different from the one on Gibbon, where Gibbon's greatness as an historian is the assumption which gives value to the minutiae of the essay's details); in fact he suggests that Voltaire was no scientist at all. What is important, however, is his 'genuine pleasure in the complexities of the universe' (p. 202). It is the excitement that is engendered by the confusing and contradictory results of Voltaire's and Madame de Chatelet's experiments that is of interest, not the potential comedy of their mistaken assumptions or their imperfect procedures. 'That the experiments were primitive, ill-directed, and unsuccessful did not trouble the investigators, and need not trouble us if we understand what they felt: they saw a new world opening in every direction and asking to be interpreted' (pp. 203–4). Although Voltaire's interpretations are finally those of a man of letters rather than a scientist (he could always turn a failed experiment into a successful *conte*), his understanding 'that the universe has not been created for our stylistic exercises' (p. 211) gives authority to his literary enterprise.

It is an enterprise, however, that is much harder to assess than Gibbon's, because it is so inextricably tied up with the man and the time. Gibbon's achievement, however much it is contained by his personality and bears the impress of his mind, exists, on another level, as totally independent of him. But, as Forster reads him, Voltaire seems to be the chief accomplishment of Voltaire, and an accomplishment, moreover, that could only have occurred when it did. 'For Voltaire, to-day, would seem a much smaller figure than he was in the eighteenth century; we should admire his personality, fear his tongue, and adore his short stories, but dismiss his "serious" utterances as journalism' (p. 209). This is a refrain that one hears in all the Voltaire essays: in the late and uncollected 'Fog over Ferney' (1958) it forms the eloquent climax. There Forster has imagined Voltaire awakening 150 years after his death and established once again at his house in Ferney. What heads of state will listen to him now? What theories can he demolish by wit and literary brilliance? Not many, for

> Ferney cannot shine far. It is too small. It sparkled on the crest of a wave which.has broken. His influence on our present world would be negligible. But would he have found our world interesting? Answer – yes. The work of Freud and of Einstein would have fascinated him, however superficial his comprehension of it. He would have popularized Einstein as he did Newton and used Freud to discredit Pascal. The knowledge that the physical universe can destroy the human race and that the human race is actually encouraging it to do so would have accorded with his cynicism and provided him with a further example of our imbecility. Perhaps it would have inspired him to write another brilliant *conte*. The spectacle of Mr Dulles, Mr K., Field-Marshal Montgomery and other contemporary giants demarcating planetary space and proceeding to eliminate their own planet from bases on Venus or Ganymede might have given even richer results than anything he had obtained from Maupertuis at Potsdam. To his lively and resilient mind the destruction of humanity would seem more than ever inevitable, but his compassion for individuals would not have ceased, nor would his curiosity. Curiosity is his message to us. Curiosity cannot avert doom, but it can act as an inoculation against fear.[32]

Compassion and curiosity were probably the cardinal virtues for Forster and it is certainly his recognition of the presence of these qualities in Voltaire that, shortly after the outbreak of the Second World War, caused Forster to choose him (along only with Shakespeare) 'to speak for Europe at the Last Judgement' – 'Shakespeare for his creative genius, Voltaire for his critical genius and humanity' (*TC*, p. 162). It is the pairing of those qualities that is crucial, just as Voltaire's irony, as we recall from the entry in the *Commonplace Book*, is powerful because of the pathos.

What makes all Forster's Voltaire essays so engaging is the sense of familiarity they project, but it is a quality that neither belittles the subject nor unduly enlarges the speaker. Voltaire may speak for him, but he is still aware of the distance between them: Voltaire's ideas 'happen to be my own . . ., and like many other small people I am thankful when a great person comes along and says for me what

I can't say properly for myself' (*TC*, p. 162). Nonetheless Voltaire, for all his belief in humanity, could be mischievous, even malicious. 'I am so fond of him that I should like to add he had a perfect character. Alas, he hadn't!' But that 'alas' is a rhetorical trick. It introduces a short catalogue of his failings (he lied, loved money too much, overdressed, had no dignity and was a tease) but in the context of the essay in which he lists these shortcomings they serve merely to emphasize Voltaire's humanity. For that essay, 'Voltaire and Frederick the Great', has as its primary concern an analysis of those qualities of human nature that are needed to resist tyranny – in particular, the German tyranny of 1941 (the date of the essay). The underlying assumption of the essay is that 'two hundred years before the Nazis came, [Voltaire] was the complete anti-Nazi'. From this point of view, Frederick is a precursor of Hitler, and Voltaire the embodiment of liberty, variety, tolerance and sympathy. 'He is not a great creative artist. But he is a great man with a powerful intellect and a warm heart, enlisted in the service of humanity' (p. 163).

If Forster's aim was, like Gibbon's, to evoke the past, his manner was, like Voltaire's, to write a *conte* – that is, to tell an essayistic tale. When Voltaire is himself the subject of such a tale, the result is more than an *hommage*; it is an act of appropriation producing a double text in which the author both judges and is judged by the subject. It is in this fashion that his own activities as a broadcaster become the indirect target of his irony in the last Voltaire essay, 'Fog over Ferney'. There, when Voltaire returns from his grave and discovers that the only head of state who is interested in receiving a letter from him is President Nehru and even that letter cannot be written in French, he takes to broadcasting instead.

> He broadcast very well, said exactly what he liked, was obscene, subversive, blasphemous, and did not discover for some time that he was speaking to a tape-recorder and that nothing was allowed on the air that might disturb the Establishment. 'La Voix de Ferney', as it was called, provided platitudinous compliments to liberty and humanitarianism, mild deism, inexplosive tolerance, and innocuous jokes.[33]

That this article was written for *The Listener*, the periodical in which many of Forster's own broadcasts had been reprinted, adds its own innocuous joke and at the same time underscores the serious argument of the essay: although latter-day Voltaires, himself included, are much dimmer figures than the original, Voltaire's genius was nonetheless tied directly to his moment in history. It is the point Forster makes in the early essays on Voltaire as scientist; it is implicit in 'Voltaire and Frederick the Great'; and it appears again in the best of the Voltaire essays, 'Ferney' (1940). The recurrent theme is scale: 'A Ferney today would have to be enormous, with rolling staircases and microphones, if it was to function proportionately, and if it was enormous could it be Ferney?' (*TC*, p. 336).

Not only is 'Ferney' the best of the Voltaire essays, it is in many ways Forster's most perfect essay.[34] It is at once a personal essay and a historical essay. Or, more precisely, it reveals the process by which the historical essay becomes the personal essay that is directly in the tradition of Montaigne, as it moves from the self to an implicit appraisal of an entire civilization. It speaks personally and politically; it is about friends and nations; it witnesses and records, assimilating both reading and experience. Its tonal range is wide – from the intimate and the comic to the meditative and tragic – and its subject matter is even wider. At its centre is a meditation on death and on the size of the universe, its pretext (and sub-text) the outbreak of the Second World War and the possible collapse of civilization.

That nearly all descriptions of Voltaire refer to him as monkey-like makes the opening of the essay comically apt: 'Cultivated monkeys, Charles and I clung to the iron palings of the park. Froggy as well as monkey, he appreciated better than I did what we saw.' The tone is casual, familiar; it gives the reader the sense of surprising an ongoing conversation among those who know, for example, that Charles is the Frenchman Charles Mauron (hence 'Froggy as well as monkey'), who know one another well enough to let their words hint at the rhythms of nursery rhymes ('this was the house that Voltaire built, those were the trees he planted' – p. 335). This familiar voice is at once substance and strategy. We are invited into a discussion on human value, a discourse on the key words, 'civilization', 'humanity', 'enjoyment', through an illustration of those very qualities. It is thus important that there be two of them clinging to the rails, that the 'humanity' that Voltaire is made to epitomize be enacted in this friendship which will have to survive despite the guarded frontiers of war. ' "I am content to have seen Ferney," remarked Charles, as he dusted his paws' (p. 338) – a sentence that must have given Forster some pain to record, as it hints not only at the oncoming global darkness, but, for the intimates of this conversation, at the impending total blindness of Mauron as well.[35]

The comical opening has a darker underside. Clinging to the railings is difficult, the parapet is uncomfortable, they are not sufficiently prehensile for their perch. Their precarious balance mimes that of their historic moment. Indeed their 'last peep at one of the symbols of European civilization' conjures up a moment that was itself a final one, for Ferney 'was too small to cope with the modern world' (p. 336). It may have 'sparkled on the crest of a wave', but after Voltaire the wave broke. As Forster writes this essay in November 1940, more than a year after his summer visit of 1939, the waves are breaking as never before. The power of the essay derives from this perspective. We are aware first of the witnesses, of the act of seeing Ferney, then of the place and the man. The essay is an urgent act of witness, for what Voltaire means are precisely those values, words, gestures, so imperilled at the moment of the essay – 'Civilization. Humanity. Enjoyment' (p. 336).

Forster constructs the essay around a double act of vision. As we watch the two friends peering at the house and grounds in 1939, we look with them at a day in 1767 when Voltaire was fêted by his friends with fireworks, plays and testimonials. The tremendous rush of details in the paragraph describing that moment is in sharp contrast to the calm emptiness of the shuttered château, where a solitary workman is sweeping up a few early leaves. This elegiac voice primarily serves a political argument. The friends were on the railings because tourists were no longer being admitted. The world was closing down for war and they were 'almost the last of [their] sinewy tribe'. 'Sinewy' at once recalls the monkey metaphor and suggests a quality the coming years will require, although it will doubtless be inadequate as 'the human make-up . . . reveal[s] deadnesses and depths which no acuteness could penetrate and no benignity heal' (p. 336).

Elegiac, however, may be an insufficient description of either voice or strategy, for the essay is not merely a lament for what may soon be lost but a paradigm for recovery. In the way the essay offers its own readings of certain received ideas, quotations or allusions as a confirmation of the validity of its own witness, it contains and objectifies that past which is imperilled at the moment of the essay. The paragraph that describes the friends peering at the chapel through the railing connects 1939 to 1767 and, through an allusion to the *Aeneid*, to 19 BC and, beyond that, to that suspended moment in Roman prehistory between empires when Aeneas in the underworld tried unavailingly to draw Dido's attention to himself and to his destiny.

The phrase *loca senta situ*, which Forster casually quotes in the second paragraph, brings with it a context at first apparently at odds with the conversationally bilingual phrase 'a trifle moisi' that he uses to describe the chapel's neglected appearance. This linking of languages is both appropriate to the way the friends must have talked, and suggestive of the difficulty of translation; there is no exact English equivalent for *moisi*. ' "Mouldy" will not do', he argues, for the chapel 'had acquired the art of neglect with dignity, and had no wish to look trim' (p. 335). But the Virgilian phrase, which indeed complicates rather than simplifies translation problems, brings in just that rejected overtone of mould and squalor ('a land rugged and forlorn' in Page's translation,[36] but, literally 'places rough with neglect or mould'). It is applied after all to the realm of the dead, and is used by Aeneas as evidence of the terrible but still ultimately unknown fate he bears. Given the larger argument of the essay, that will turn out to be precisely the right note, but here a gap remains between allusion and context. For the essay has yet to bring into direct collision the two last moments that are its subject – the end of Ferney and possibly the end of the writer's world.

It is curious, even so, that Forster never tried out the translation 'mossy', even if that is not the precise equivalent (the problem is more one of concept than of language; the affective connotations of 'mossy' have no echo in French). Perhaps he mentions 'mouldy' because he already had the phrase from Virgil in mind as aptly portentous of this time and place, and he wanted both to use it and to limit its suggestiveness. The phrase remains problematic, however, in so far as it calls attention to the difficulties of language. It opens up a gap in the text that mimes the actual one it records, i.e. the separation of friends, the sealing of borders. Thus the saving-up of fragments (the visit itself being one such fragment: 'I popped the object into my pouch for future use' – p. 338) becomes a necessary (and a restorative) response to a world on the verge of disintegration.

The phrase from the *Aeneid* is not the only piece of the past embedded in the essay. One quotation, cited as a commonplace by 'the spirit of dullness', 'Count no man happy until he is dead' (p.

336), trails a long history after it as it passes through Sophocles and Herodotus, Cicero and Ovid, and, most interestingly for Forster's purposes, Montaigne. It is both the phrase itself and the reverberations that it sets up in its context that make this act of quotation so very Montaigne-like. For Montaigne, this 'commonplace' is directly the subject of two early essays (I.19–20) in which he seems to be subscribing to that pious belief, but, in the context of the three volumes and multiple revisions of the *Essais*, the statement becomes ever more problematic and is, in fact, often directly challenged ('it is in a happy life, not . . . in a happy death, that human felicity consists' – 'On Repentance';[37] or '[death] is indeed the end but not the aim of life' – 'On Physiognomy'[38]). Forster, like Montaigne, used such statements as essayistic occasions. Here the commonplace becomes a means to test the facts of Voltaire's life and to structure a reading of that life in order to focus a critical moral issue, one that takes on an added edge in the wartime darkness:

> His end was actually at Paris, and technically not happy. 'Count no man happy until he is dead', saith the spirit of dullness. Happiness up to one's final collapse is the better criterion, and this Voltaire achieved. The pains and fears of his last moments (which most of us are doomed to share) altered the sum of his life but inappreciably. The death-bed or death-tumble or death-jumble, death-battle, death-rattle, death-splinter, death-squirt, appalling as it will be to each deserted and dying individual, is a transition, not an epitome. It has no retrospective force. It does not taint (except in a gleam of diseased memory) any of the triumphs that have gone before. Against that over-emphasis, that priestly organization of the death-moment, Voltaire had himself protested, it was part of the infamous thing he had tried to crush. His real end was Ferney, and there we saw him that afternoon, as a house and trees.   (*TC*, pp. 336–7)

This is a complex passage, for several arguments are proceeding simultaneously. The actual facts of Voltaire's death both confirm and deny commonplace assumptions. And it is just those assumptions that Forster challenges in a rhetorical flourish that is to prose what 'death be not proud' is to poetry. In his passion and scorn, Forster assumes the Voltaire persona as he merges subject and object, or, perhaps more accurately, as he constitutes his speaking self out of his subject. Indeed, by the end of the paragraph, the Ferney that Voltaire inhabited and the Ferney that Forster and Mauron saw as the last witnesses of a last moment are indistinguishable, just as Voltaire's anti-clericalism is stated in Forster's own attack on the 'priestly organization of the death-moment'.

It is in his use of quotation and in the way he assimilated his subject's voice to his own that Forster demonstrated his indebtedness to Montaigne. And it is Montaigne, we must recall, who in 'What I Believe' is named, along with Erasmus, as one of Forster's law-givers. Rather than Strachey, with whom Forster did not share much more than a certain idiom and an occasional likeness of tone, it is Montaigne and Gibbon and Voltaire who provide the essential reference points for Forster's essays. But Montaigne is not so much an influence as an implicit presence whose *Essais* constitute an important intertext for the reading of much of Forster's non-fiction writing.

6

From Private Self to Public Text

I THE *COMMONPLACE BOOK* AS *ESSAI*

The essential strategy of the historical essays remained constant throughout Forster's writing career, although as the Second World War approached an apocalyptic note was struck that had not sounded before. From 'Cnidus' to 'Voltaire and Frederick the Great', some person, place or time is evoked, examined, 'read'; it is made to test and is itself tested by the speaker's unfolding beliefs, which are both embedded in the expository language and detachable as direct statement. As a result, the essays are at once intensely personal and impersonal; they begin with the self, but they move outward from the self. Rereading *The Decline and Fall* 'to find parallels between the collapse of the Mediterranean civilization . . . and the apparent collapse of world civilization today', Forster discovers that parallels do not exist, but he finds the act of looking back into history still to be useful, for 'I do think it strengthens our outlook occasionally to glance into the past, and to lift our eyes from the wave that threatens to drown us to the great horizons of the sea of history, where personal safety no longer signifies' (*TC*, p. 157).

This last sentence reveals Forster in a most characteristic stance; he is reading at the threshold of writing. As he reads, he appropriates the text by refiguring it, in this instance in the metaphor of the sea with Gibbon the 'great navigator' and the work 'a well-built ship'. This should not be considered simply fancy or fanciful writing on Forster's part, for it allows him both to hold on to Gibbon's text and to fashion his own, even when that prior text does not yield the precise consolation or confirmation he needs amid the horrors of 1942. Through his language he is able to give scale to his own experience. Words such as 'occasionally' and 'glance' suggest a world still in our power, while the phrase 'the wave that threatens to drown' challenges that apparent control. But even when quotation fails, when no prior words can chart the present moment, the act of

94

reading is itself affirmed. And the human scale of that reading holds even beneath those 'great horizons', as the last part of the sentence, in its conversational easiness, evokes a particular, almost intimate, human voice, although one that refuses any merely self-interested point of view.

It is this figure of Forster reading that I want to examine now, but earlier, at that juncture when he is remaking himself as a writer. One can date this moment precisely, 21 October 1925, the day he took down Bishop Jebb's *Commonplace Book*, defined 'commonplaces' as his first entry, and began a project of enormous significance for all his future writing. How calculated or fortuitous this moment was it is impossible to know. In retrospect it seems almost unavoidable. It clearly marks the beginning of the transformation of Forster the novelist into a different kind of writer. In it he begins the construction of a textual self whose public texts are the essays and broadcasts, collected and uncollected, that he wrote over the following three decades and which, taken together, constitute an extraordinary and demanding body of prose.

The first thing he notes in his commonplace about commonplaces is his difficulty in making them, since 'I shall not know what they are about until they are finished'. Unlike the bishop whose precedent he is attempting to follow, he does not have 'certified topics' that he can 'carry about intact': 'I must know what is inside me before I can tell what I am after' (*CB*, p. 1). It is no wonder, then, that three entries later he announces a 'change of plan', for the bishop's scheme, a topic word followed by a rounded paragraph or two, is far too determined and closed a form for that open-ended musing that might not even discover its subject before it was done. Not that Forster cannot write within such a constraint. The third entry, 'Resentment', an anatomy of his response to Middleton Murry's attacks, is totally self-contained. It is reflective, self-aware, ironic at his own expense and at the same time it objectifies its insight and enlarges the issue far beyond a quarrel between two literary men. But the very accomplishment of this entry might have given him pause as if it were too demanding a precedent. Would every entry be able to move so neatly to closure? Could every entry develop with such strict dependence on a generating word? He thinks not and decides to 'put down whatever I like' (p. 2), keeping the appearance intact – he will still underline the first word and let it protrude over the margin – but he will let the book take its own shape and find its own voice.

Having declared this new purpose, he is for a while silent. When he returns to the volume it is to work out his reading for the Clark Lectures that were to become *Aspects of the Novel*.[1] The entries are for the most part impersonal – quotations, assessments, the construction of a system of classification that will be helpful and avoid pedantries: 'my temperament is to dismiss all this sort of stuff as the product of the examination-system . . . the desire to appear weighty often disguises itself as disinterested curiosity' (p. 11). He thus explores both his materials and his own subjectivity and he looks for ways to test the validity or accuracy of his judgements. He is obviously using the *Commonplace Book* in part for the traditional purpose of anthologizing useful passages, and it is a function the book will continue to perform over the years, but he has still not really begun it. It is only after the Lectures that it properly begins, when his reading, like Montaigne's, becomes a means of discovering who he is, and how he thinks. He proceeds there as Montaigne claims he did in his essays – taking advantage of every occasion, taking the first subject chance offers, giving himself up to doubt and uncertainty, 'and to my predominant quality, which is ignorance' (Montaigne, I.50, p. 290; p. 131[2]).

It would be very nice now to be able to turn to a Forster essay on Montaigne or at least to a *Commonplace Book* entry or to a letter or diary passage on the essayist, but no such text exists. The few extant remarks of Forster on Montaigne are significant, however. In the most famous one, in 'What I Believe' (1938), Forster calls Montaigne his 'law giver', opposing him and Erasmus to those other law-givers, the emblematic figures of orthodoxy and faith, 'Moses and St Paul' (*TC*, p. 65). The same pairing occurs three years later in 'Tolerance' when Forster scans history for 'great men who have recommended tolerance. St Paul certainly did not. Nor did Dante.' However, Erasmus did, and 'in the same century there was the Frenchman Montaigne, subtle, intelligent, witty, who lived in his quiet country house and wrote essays which still delight and confirm the civilized' (*TC*, p. 46). 'Civilized' is no accidental word in that context, at that moment. As all the essays of the late thirties and early forties insist, civilization is in danger, and not only by assaults from without. Confirming civilization is the first step in the rebuilding process that will eventually be necessary, although not so soon as Forster had anticipated in 1941.

But the most significant aspect of that last statement for my purposes is Forster's linking of living and writing as he thinks about

Montaigne. For what Montaigne accomplished above all was the simultaneous invention of a new consciousness *and* a new genre. In inventing his life he invented a text; or perhaps it was the other way around, for it is impossible to establish the priority of either accomplishment. In Montaigne's 'To the Reader', which appeared as preface to the first two volumes of *Essais*, this becomes clear at once: 'it is myself that I portray . . . I am myself the substance of my book.' And in one of the most interesting of the essays in the second volume, 'On Presumption', he replies to the question of his imaginary interlocutor (himself) – 'for whom are you writing?' (II.17, p. 640; p. 218) – by making himself not only the originator and subject of his text, but its audience as well.[3] 'The world always looks outward, I turn my gaze inward; there I fix it and there I keep it busy. Everyone looks before him; I look within. I have no business but with myself' (II.17, p. 641; p. 219). Although such statements would seem to blur the boundary between self and text, making it difficult to know exactly what either means or says, the *Essais* from the start were read in an anthologizing fashion, as if both categories were fixed, permanent and totally knowable. 'Wise sayings' were culled and published in extracts; the 'thought' was arranged in neat thematic categories. Such a reading procedure not only took in a peculiarly literal way the asserted link between writer and writing by subordinating the text to the historical figure, but it also gave a falsely fixed character to the thought itself, much of which was not even Montaigne's, but the commonplaces of an already much anthologized classical past.

However, Forster's reading of Montaigne was not, I would suggest, a particularly anthologizing one; he certainly did not cull sayings from the *Essais* for *his* commonplace book. When he called Montaigne his law-giver, he was referring not to any set of statements–laws that he had extracted in his reading, but to an attitude of mind that was not bound by received pieties or precepts. It is the solitary figure of Montaigne, alone with his books and his thoughts, that he offered as a counterweight to that headlong rush into belief that characterized the bloody Age of Faith he found himself living in. But the reflective/reflexive, self-regarding/self-effacing act of living/writing that Montaigne originated came to Forster in highly problematic terms. He could use Montaigne as a tonic, fortifying him to resist a world of rigid creeds, of state-sanctioned beliefs, but what could he make of him for himself; how could he constitute himself in the terms Montaigne offered; what of

Montaigne was available to him in his belatedness? For Forster clearly was and, indeed, saw himself as, the end product of the humanist tradition that Montaigne had 'invented'. Forster could write subtle, witty essays, but what could they 'confirm' in a present when 'liberalism . . . [is] crumbling' (*TC*, p. 72) and humanism itself in danger of becoming the sort of reified creed that it supplanted?

Attempting to answer this last question is crucial for a reading of the essays of the thirties and forties. But before that public Forster (very public indeed, as many of the essays were originally broadcasts) can be adequately confronted, the more private writer, essaying his new persona of the critic–commentator, should be encountered. The *Commonplace Book*, situated precisely on the borderline between private text (diary, letter) and public text (lecture, broadcast, essay), provides the space for just such an encounter.

It is indeed physically very much a book – a large, impressive book, 'bound in boards and strong quarter-calf'.[4] When Forster decided to continue it, he found the leather cracked 'like much else in my time', a difficulty had he wished to hand it on, but bequests and such traditions were coming to an end – 'there is not time for the personal memory-sogged past' (*TC*, p. 181). So Forster with no posterity save his books (Montaigne: 'I do not know whether I would not much rather have produced a perfectly formed child by intercourse with the Muses than by intercourse with my wife' – 'On the Affection of Fathers for their Children', ii.8, p. 383; pp. 157–8) re-enters the world of such traditions. He is ironically aware of how remote from him it is, but he knows as well that he must find some access to it if he is fully to inhabit his present. It is no accident that this undertaking occurs at the same time as he moves into a family house (the one his father had built for his aunt), but one that is only temporarily to be his, and one which he can live in only by simultaneously not living there, by taking a London flat, both for his own privacy and to satisfy an impulse not to be rooted, or countrified or contained. The external circumstances – the discovery of the book, the wanted/unwanted inheritance of property – are obliquely reflected in the contents of the book itself. The dominant tone, however, is far from 'memory-sogged'. Indeed, if any single impulse is most strenuously resisted, it is the tendency to prettify and halo the past.

The entries are endlessly revealing, and even the relatively tired or dutiful ones often contain brilliant and unsettling lines. They can be read, as can the letters, for their choice bits, their aphoristic gleams. But they are more interesting and more moving when read as a text of process – that is, when read as we read Montaigne's *Essais*, seeing each essay as a 'trial of judgement' (1.50, p. 289; p. 130), discrete but endlessly open to revision, a record of his life's *essais* ('un registre des essais de ma vie', usually translated as 'experiences' – III.13, p. 1056; p. 361) as essay. Forster hardly 'discovered' the essay form, but he did discover his own essayistic voice. Unlike Montaigne, however, he was creating himself not *ab ovo*, but out of a prior (and, for him, privileged) genre. Thus the most complex process these entries reveal is the discovery of the essayistic voice as a function of his engagement first with history and then with fiction – the novel of the past 200 years and his own novels and stories.

The early entries – those written between 1926 and 1929 – demonstrate the second half of this proposition very clearly. Not only is Forster working out his argument for *Aspects*, but he is also looking for the sources of a new novel within his own experience, both intellectual and emotional. He is at the same time wary of experience, not least of all because it can be so readily falsified by words, particularly by the act of writing:

Literature as Compensation   'I shall make something out of this some day' must have occurred to many an unhappy man of letters, and to *have* made something is possible – Heine, A. E. Housman, Shakespeare avow it. But to cherish the hope implies a vulgarity of mind, the writing habit, the innate though unacknowledged faith that things in a book aren't so real, so that if anything agonising happens the first impulse is to regard it bookishly and blunt its edge. 'The higher reality of art?' Yes, it exists, but the above is its counterfeit. – Literature, literature, literature, for the last fortnight I can't stick it, its 1) self-expression, 2) aesthetic, 3) deals with personal relationships, by-products all. I want expression, not self-expression. To add to the number of people who write down what they feel about a sunset or two imaginary characters in a bed together, is an ignoble profession, as soon as one sees its ignobility: all right as long as pursued naïvely.

Well one way and another, the writing down and printing of human words seems doomed to decay spiritually.

What I write down here is itself tainted by the hope of gaining relief from my pain.

Pain always includes insincerity.

Sympathy $\left.\right\}$ brings the insincerity out
Self pity

After writing this commonplace I feel less pain. Anything does, even if trying to be truthful. By describing what has happened one gets away from what happened.   (*CB*, pp. 47–8)

The entry is itself an illustration of its point in so far as it circles in a series of revisions to an acknowledgement via contradiction of its main assertion. It is in a sense a version of the paradox of the Cretan liar: the entry is 'tainted' by the admission that writing it has relieved pain and pain is 'tainted' by its implicit 'insincerity'. Forster writes here to forestall writing. He is looking for a literary form that would predict its own insufficiency and failure.

This is a procedure very like Montaigne's in the way it essays its conclusions, but in one assumption there is a marked difference. For Montaigne, expression means self-expression; indeed there is no way to distinguish between the two. But Forster, more consciously elusive, wants to find a writing that both inscribes and conceals him – 'expression, not self-expression'. (One needs to recall, however, that in fact Montaigne is infinitely elusive, despite his frequent assertions that he writes only to reveal himself, and Forster in an entry on his supposed elusiveness claims surprise at the label, even as his concluding sentence seems to acknowledge it: 'Supposed an elf, I am actually a ——' – p. 31.) Forster's writing is implicitly autobiographical, but in a deflected, partially allegorized form. It is a more accurate record of emotion than of incident, and its strategies are those of concealment rather than revelation.

Even the novel that he proposes beginning is to be an exercise in 'expression, not self-expression': '*Novel, beginning one*' (p. 28). It will be about himself, 'a *middle-aged* novel, i.e. by myself as an M. A.', and it will be generated out of a specific emotion, the contemplation of 'the shades of the prison house', for 'to realise our passions have become habits has itself the force of a passion'. He will try to 'get down the first hand experiences of [his] life'. But the problem that arises here is very close to that in the entry 'Literature as Compensation': he itemizes the events of his day but realizes that he could have spent the identical day twenty years earlier – 'Digested by my literary mind, it will tend to reappear as a young man's day, and all the incidents will be haloed with a spurious novelty & wonder' (p. 29). He approaches the problem from several directions, but it remains intractable, how to 'transfer . . . on to paper experiences (which however ardent and insistent are not new) without giving them a spurious newness and making them booky' (p. 30).

But this is not an issue that is only raised here and then dropped. Indeed, in reading the *Commonplace Book* one must engage not simply the entry but the context as well; in particular, it helps to observe how an entry can give rise to others and provide context and commentary. For example, in 'Public Bores', two entries before the one on beginning a novel, he lists some bores in a half-serious, half-playful fashion: for example, H. M. Tomlinson, Cunninghame Graham, but also 'Edward Thompson of Boars Hill itself, though he cannot be counted among true boars until borne in silence. Baughan-Williams?' (p. 27). The list expands, he imagines an essay on 'the emasculation of the public mind' and speculates on the responsibility of education and educators, on whether there is a 'connection or antithesis between education and creation', and then on the connection between influence and merit. The next entry is labelled 'Time' and contains a quotation from *The Magic Mountain* with the notation that it is 'expressed from a poetical standpoint though not poetically'. It would seem that there has been a complete change of subject, but then follows a note on Mann as a 'bore, but from a sense of literary duty rather than personally'. He follows this with an expansion of his assessment of Mann's style in contrast to his own and then moves to the next entry, on beginning a novel. This entry, he remarks midway, was prompted by his reading Mann and his observing how both Mann and Conrad face his problem, i.e. the search for ways to avoid the 'high threnodic note' (*CB*, p. 30), a problem that is further complicated by his desire at the same time to avoid 'too close contact with H. J. [Henry James]' (p. 29). Reading Mann is essentially responsible for each of these entries. Although the subjects seem separate, they circle not only around a common text, but also around a common preoccupation: is there a new novel available to him or is he too exhausted both in spiritual and literary terms to write one? The anxious conclusion to the 'Time' entry is significant. As he thinks of Mann, he observes that 'the German never gives that anxious look behind to see whether trails of unnecessary words are not clinging to his skirts – an anxious look habitual with me, and entailing expenditure of vitality which might have been employed otherwise' (p. 28). The fear of 'loss of vitality' one might call his Henry James worry, the 'unnecessary words', his sense of the possibilities of the Mann way, even at the risk of being a bore. Hence the concluding exhortation to himself: 'be very tolerant with bores who have something to say. If they did not bore they might not say it.'

The *Commonplace Book* is thus a testing ground for both his creative and his critical selves. It is a record of reading and experience as sources of writing. But how to keep the one from contaminating the other, how to write a book that remains a day, not a literary day, not some recollection in tranquillity, but the day itself? There is a possible answer, and he attempts to pursue it, to find a literature 'unbothered by sunsets' (p. 46) where he can jettison that 'ruck-sack of traditional nature-emotions' (p. 40) which weighs down on him so heavily. Thus he reads Eddington, both *Stars and Atoms* and *The Nature of the Physical World*, and copies out extracts as they provoke reflections on the relationship between love and lust, on the unstable nature of friendship, on the 'philosophic pretentiousness' (*CB*, p. 46) of literature. And he tries, as he elsewhere does with what he identifies as the purely aesthetic approach of Fry and to a lesser degree of Woolf, to turn his habitual response to nature (a response which seems to generate both subject and incident as well as provide the dominant coloration) away from the self, and to fix it in some external reality. He senses his failure, however, with both the scientific and aesthetic approaches: 'Here, as with the bacteria, I am at the frontiers of a kingdom but cannot get in' (p. 40). If he cannot make the new science yield a new literature, he still tries to make it yield a kind of consolation, a means of 'steering through disappointments and betrayals', although he had earlier cautioned against this loosely metaphoric sort of reading. However, just as he begins to take himself too seriously he turns the PS of the entry into 'Pee Shit' and remarks that 'all this went fut in a day or two' (p. 47). It would have had to, given one of his conclusions derived from Eddington, 'the seriousness of a large housefly can't be taken too seriously' (p. 46).

Reading and writing imply each other; out of the two activities a self emerges. It is quite consciously fashioned although not always completely approved of by its creator, who is ironically aware of its 'housefly' limitations. Nonetheless he lets it buzz, and on subjects more varied than the problem of the writer. However, even those entries that are primarily note-taking for an external occasion, the lecture tour for Ibsen's centenary, for example, provide an occasion for an implicit self-scrutiny. That is, preoccupied with his own creative problems, he is alert to those aspects of Ibsen that echo or imply them. He identifies a thematic emphasis in *Peer Gynt*, *'salvation by being loved'*, in a way that suggests his own preoccupations, remarking that the play is really 'a poem pretending to be a sermon', despite Ibsen's avowed purpose (*CB*, p. 35). He particularly notes the process whereby the 'past recurs as a half sentence during a moment of crisis, or insinuates itself into an apparently straight line of thought' – all observations that have obvious application to his own writing.

Some entries, however, simply propose an interesting text as it may contain a phrasing or an idea that strikes his fancy and does not require much by way of comment or application. And in some entries the emphasis is on the act of reading itself, not on what the words 'say'. An entry called 'Dryden's Epistles' provides a very nice example. Three stanzas are copied out – very carefully and neatly, complete with Dryden's marginalia – followed by two notes that reflect the act of reading and copying:

> Reading these Epistles which have no connection with my 'work' and little with my ideas, have [*sic*] given me a happy sense of my own leisure. Who has the necessary time and vacancy of mind to read Dryden's Epistles for pleasure in 1927? or to copy out extracts from them into a Commonplace Book? Or to write out more often than is necessary the words: Dryden, Epistles, Dryden's Epistles? No one but me and perhaps Siegfried Sassoon.
>
> An hour with Dryden's Epistles read for pleasure.
>
> September night windy, dark, warm and I have read the Epistles of John Dryden.   (p. 27)

Such an entry seems almost purely objective, untouched by any appropriating or transforming commentary, but it is, in fact, the most subjective of all, as it concentrates so utterly on the reader as subject.

It is, I would suggest, in this concentration on the act of reading that the relationship to Montaigne can be most clearly felt. For Montaigne constantly wrote through others, inscribing himself in the other text. On the one hand he claimed that what he wrote was merely a means of transmitting the thoughts of others: 'my book is constructed wholly of spoils taken from them' (ii.32, p. 699; p. 227).

On the other, he understood the degree to which his borrowings were transformed merely by the act of quotation: 'I prefer to twist a good saying in order to weave it into my argument, rather than twist my argument to receive it' (1.26, p. 171; p. 79). Or, 'Amongst so many borrowings, I am glad if I can occasionally steal something to disguise and adapt for a new service' (III.12, p. 1034; p. 335).[5] It is not that Forster was writing through Dryden or in any sense adapting him to his purpose, as Montaigne did with his 'sources', but he did use the act of reading Dryden as a way of talking about the self while talking about something else. Furthermore, as he explains in the 1940 essay on Bishop Jebb's *Commonplace Book*, he often used the Montaigne tactic of ventriloquism. Referring to the bishop's use of quotation, he remarked, 'his spirit also saves me from scandal: we both tend to be non-intimate on the subjects of letters and life, and to saddle Seneca or Ibsen with anything which we do not quite want to say' (*TC*, p. 183). And then, in a Montaigne-like contradiction: 'It would do his reputation no harm if the whole collection was published, and mine no good.'

One acquiesces without difficulty in this suggestion of reticence and self-concealment; it is an obvious quality of all the fiction and many of the essays. But, curiously, despite the specific claim Forster is making here, it is not really a characteristic of the *Commonplace Book* – hence the potential scandal. True, he does not here, as he does in letters and diaries, speak specifically of people and incidents, but an intimate portrait of a mind, and, incidentally, of a body does clearly emerge. Indeed there are certain topics that, in their recurrence over the years (and here I am speaking of the book in its full forty-year span and not the initial three years isolated earlier), constitute a kind of refrain. They are: memory, friendship, the body and death. And, as a reader of Montaigne will instantly recognize, these four topics provide the thematic co-ordinates for the *Essais* as well.

One way in which Montaigne makes good his claim that he is his book, that he 'communicate[s] with the world . . . with his whole being' (III.2, p. 782; p. 236), is by using his body as text – his digestion, his excretions, his infamous stone. Textual *essai* and life's *essais* are the same – 'I study myself more than any other subject. This is my metaphysics, this is my physics' (III.13, p. 1050; p. 353).[6] The physical is omnipresent: the body is anatomized, examined in detail, described for the pleasure of it and made to generate much of the 'purely' speculative discourse. Thus the observation that 'life is an unequal, irregular, and multiform movement' (III.3, p. 796; p. 251), which he makes in the essay 'Of Three Kinds of Relationships' (friendship, sex, books), can be readily invoked to sanction not only the choice of subjects, but the formal, generic experiment as well. It is a statement that, more than any other of the numerous self-describing statements that Montaigne makes, comes closest to encompassing the entire project. It can also be applied directly to the Forster of the *Commonplace Book* as he examines books, friendships, bodily functions, bodily desires, dreams, places, ideas. In these entries the essayist's persona is tried/essayed; his readings are made to yield both a portrait of the reader and the subjects of that reader's speculations. Taken together they constitute the matter and, to a degree, the manner of the published essays.

Two of these essays, written only months after Forster began the *Commonplace Book*, clearly suggest affinities with the kinds of writing he was trying out there and, in their use of the body–text equivalence, reveal him in the Montaigne-like stance of self-making as well. 'Me, Them and You' and 'My Wood' are both meditations on experience that are played off against the fragments of Forster's reading and literary memory.[7] At the same time they reveal a strong narrative impulse, especially in their creation of an essay 'I' who both constructs and is the subject. This 'I' illustrates the essay's argument by literally embodying it (in the sense that his body becomes each text's central image). But by using a voice that is distinct from this 'embodying' – that is, by speaking to his fictive self – he creates an ironic space for commentary and correction.

'My Wood' provides by far the denser tissue of commonplaces: three from Scripture (Matthew 19:24; 24:27; Luke 16:19–23), one from Shakespeare, one from Dante. It is through them that the text's central question is posed: 'what is the effect of property upon the character?', the public question that is then rephrased as 'what's the effect on me of my wood?' (where both word order and contracted verb form also reflect this shift in focus – *AH*, p. 23). These commonplaces are used in a curious way, however. They are essentially inverted, in that their depiction of the deformities that possession imposes on the human spirit is accepted but (at least for the scriptural allusions) not their programme. Indeed, just the reverse, for the entire essay derives from the two-edged assumption that 'our life on earth is, and ought to be, material and carnal. But we have not yet learned to manage our materialism and carnality properly; they are still entangled with the desire for ownership' (p.

25). This statement is interesting as it prefigures what Forster will two decades later, in 'The Challenge of our Time', describe as the problem he cannot 'equate'. However, here it is less logically argued than fictionally imagined through a narrative procedure that is closer to story than to essay.

The essay constructs its analysis around a character who is both the same as and distinct from the essay's speaker, a grotesque creation who is depicted at the close as 'enormously stout, endlessly avaricious, pseudo-creative, [and] intensely selfish' (p. 26). But the 'I' is split; the visual image kept separate from voice. As the figurative character swells, the voicing character deflates. As that grotesque figure enacts the literal significance of each of the essay's commonplaces, the essayistic voice translates and generalizes them in a rhetorical procedure that merges ornate visual figuration with a verbal plain style: property 'produces men of weight. Men of weight cannot, by definition, move like the lightning from the East unto the West, and the ascent of a fourteen-stone bishop into a pulpit is thus the exact antithesis of the coming of the Son of Man' (p. 24).

The two exemplary figures that flank the 'I' in a triptych arrangement suggest this stylistic range as well – the Man from Lyme Regis and *his* wood and Dives in Hell. So do the blackberries, the final image for the problem of property and possession: blackberries that are seen from the public footpath and gathered; that are seen along with foxgloves and toadstools, similarly gathered; that are seen along with lovers rolling in the bracken, and tins and paper – a comic catalogue that belongs to the voice that primly inquires, 'pray, does my wood belong to me or doesn't it?' The Man from Lyme Regis solved the problem by building 'high stone walls each side of [his] path' (p. 25); yet even Dives in Hell, the very eponym of wealth and property, seems to have had the better part, for 'the gulf dividing him from Lazarus could be traversed by vision', but the stone walls in the Lyme Regis wood block out even that: 'nothing traverses it here' (p. 26). Between these two figures looms the 'enormously stout' shape of the essay's subject, a mute embodiment of the potential deformities of the speaker's moral being.

The narrator's body, both naked and clothed, also provides the central image of 'Me, Them and You'. And at that essay's centre, as in 'My Wood', is the verb 'entangled', an apt metonym for both essays: 'Me, Them and You' speaks of 'the snobbery and glitter in which our souls and bodies have been entangled' (*AH*, p. 30); 'My

Wood', of 'our materialism and carnality . . . still entangled with the desire for ownership' (p. 25). 'Me, Them and You' is also built upon a commonplace, a single statement from Carlyle: 'Thou wert our conscript, on Thee the lot fell. . . . For in Thee also a godlike frame lay hidden, but it was not to be unfolded' (p. 30).[8] In this essay, Teufelsdrockh's apostrophe from *Sartor Resartus* finds its embodiment in a painting that provides both the essay's occasion and its visual text.

The essays are further related through their use of allegory. In 'My Wood' each spiritual deformity is given an image and a name and assigned a role in a structure that moves like a morality play where the arena is the narrator's soul. But the controlling voice, in its urbanity and comic sense of the incongruous, so dominates that the allegorical and didactic are distanced. By contrast, in 'Me, Them and You', allegory provides the dominant mode, the narrating voice split among the essay's personifications. The narrator speaks as 'me', as 'you' and as 'them', but, when he speaks as 'us', 'you', the Carlylean subject, is rendered mute; the sense of human solidarity that the essay had attempted to construct is dispersed by an awareness of the gulf between 'us' and 'you'.

The essay is constructed around a double action: going to an exhibit of Sargent paintings of the rich and the mighty, and reading those paintings. But the first is not simply the frame: it is part of the social decorum that provides the narrative content of the second. For having the one shilling and sixpence that is the price of admission and having the clothes that make 'me' one of 'them', even if only distantly, are the conditions that allow the readings in the first place. However, the more the narrator 'reads', the more distant he feels from 'them', as these portraits seem to chorus,

> 'What would the country do without us? . . . we have the largest houses and eat the best food, . . . and breed the most valuable children, and ours is the Kingdom and the Power and the Glory.' And, listening to their chorus, I felt this was so, and my clothes fitted worse and worse.   (*AH*, pp. 28–9)

It is suddenly coming upon the painting *Gassed*, however, with its lying and sanitized depiction of a battlefield, that shocks the narrator into an awareness of his implicit and complicit relationship with 'them'. Such a painting could only be included in this exhibit because of its dishonesty, its telling of a 'new sort of lie' (p. 29), a lie, moreover, that confirms the self-serving and sentimental illusions of the portraits on the wall. As they look at the battle painting, they are 'still able to say, "how touching", instead of "how obscene" '. The spectator can see this, but he knows the degree of his own complicity, and realizes the enormous distance between 'him' and 'you', the soldiers depicted there, for he is quite unsentimentally aware that 'you are the slush and dirt on which our civilization rests', and 'you' are not just the doomed youth, but 'old men and women and dirty babies also' (p. 29).

The essay, however, is not a tract with a programme. Although it is an implicit critique of the ideology of class, it restricts its focus to an exploration of the boundaries of the social self, to a discourse on clothes as they constitute the self, and on the attempt to make a claim for the self that is not determined by those clothes, that has no ready identification as 'me', 'them', 'you'. The attempt fails. The narrator leaves the portraits still speaking on the wall of privilege and power, and, in a sharp break with the voice of the preceding pages, he ventriloquizes a new voice for 'us' in which 'our' needs and 'yours' merge in a rhetoric that derives from the language of late-nineteenth-century radicalism and twentieth-century political propaganda: 'far away, in some other category, far away from the snobbery and glitter in which our souls and bodies have been entangled, is forged the instrument of the new dawn' (p. 30). It is a strategy that Forster several times used in the short stories – 'Other Kingdom' and 'The Story of a Panic' are the most obvious examples – a shifting of key in which the realistic details of the fiction are restated in a prophetic mode. The more usual essay strategy, by contrast, is a scaling down, a returning of the subject to the experiencing self. One can readily see this in the later essay 'What I Believe', which concludes with a figure that also depends on the speaker as body: 'Naked I came into the world, naked I shall go out of it! And a very good thing too, for it reminds me that I am naked under my shirt, whatever its colour' (*TC*, p. 73).

The sense of the self as body is implicit in many of Forster's essays. And, in that concluding line from 'What I Believe', the specificity of the allusion to blackshirts or brownshirts aside, one can almost hear the voice of Montaigne, despite the enormous gap between the sixteenth-century originator and his twentieth-century heir. Both writers, indeed, speak out of amazingly similar preoccupations and with voices that have multiple resonances for each other. In a 1927 'Memory Note' in his *Commonplace Book*, for example, Forster described the forgetting and then the process of attempting to recall three names (a plant, a writer, a title); he added a marginal note twelve years later reiterating his difficulty in remembering one of the names (p. 32). Montaigne, too, was always chasing in his memory for the fragments he had forgotten: 'if I press it it becomes bewildered . . . it serves me at its own hours, not at mine' (ii.17, p. 633; p. 210). Yet the writing of both is saturated in memory, evidence of the complex process of recuperation that writing imposes on reading and experience. They both, also, as I suggested in the last chapter, recur frequently to death and dying, testing the old commonplaces with a similar suspicion of the priestly function. But it is in their discussions of friendship that the most profound likeness can be discovered. It is not immediately obvious, for example, that it was Montaigne and *not* Forster who wrote, 'a unique and dominant friendship dissolves all other obligations' (1.28, p. 190; p. 101). Small wonder that Forster should have called Montaigne his 'law giver' in the same essay in which he wrote, 'I hate the idea of causes, and if I had to choose between betraying my country and betraying my friend I hope I should have the guts to betray my country' (*TC*, p. 66).

II 'TO TALK THIS LATE NINETEEN CENTURY STUFF WITH A TWENTY CENTURY VOICE'

Early in 1940, reading Lord Acton's *The Study of History*, Forster composed an essay-entry in his *Commonplace Book* that, in its handling of Acton's text, provides both a model for reading Forster's own essays, especially the political ones of the Second World War period, and a conceptual framework for assessing them:

'*A speech of Antigone*, a single sentence of Socrates, a few lines that were inscribed on an Indian rock before the Second Punic War, the footsteps of a silent yet prophetic people who dwelt by the Dead Sea, and perished in the fall of Jerusalem, come nearer to our lives than the ancestral wisdom of barbarians who fed their swine on the Hercynian acorns.'

Finely put, O Lord Acton, but nearer to whose lives? This afternoon (29–2–40) I was at Bishops Cross, where new born lambs were dying in the cold, and Hughie Waterston, a Nazi by temperament, was trying to save them[.] He had put one of them in a bucket over a valor-perfection lamp. Him the ancestral wisdom inspired. Lord Acton is right, but by a much narrower margin than he supposed. He forgot that most people do not respond to culture or intellectual honesty. He forgot that there was something irresponsive to them even in himself. Ignoring social variety, neglectful of psychology, he appears, to this generation as an old man lecturing in a cap and gown. What he said was true yet it can be written the other way round, and not make nonsense, and it is always so written in Germany. I will so write it myself: he would not disapprove of the exercise: –

'The ancestral wisdom of barbarians who fed their swine on the Hercynian acorns comes nearer to our lives than a speech of Antigone, a single sentence of Socrates, a few lines that were inscribed on an Indian rock before the Second Punic War, the footsteps of a silent yet prophetic people who dwelt by the Dead Sea and perished in the fall of Jerusalem.'

This is the first time I have used my mind today; day of inertia and of waiting for the end. Yet my duty is plain enough: to talk this late nineteen century stuff with a twenty century voice and not be shoved out of believing in intellectual honesty and in the individual . . . .   (*CB*, pp. 117–18)

For Forster there could be no exchange of the *Antigone* for some Hercynian acorns; that play was a touchstone of value for him – 'of all the great tragic utterances that comes closest to my heart, that is my central faith' ('A Book that Influenced Me' [1944], *TC*, p. 215). Yet he was willing to render so central a faith problematic, if by an at least temporary suspension of certainty he could test it against the not so easily readable flux of experience and personal loyalties. For Hughie Waterston was a friend – a 'Nazi by temperament', but nonetheless deeply connected to his life. 'Hughie Waterson left last week. . . . We are going to miss one another.' This in a letter to William Plomer, in which the sentences that follow provide a suggestive gloss for the passage under consideration: 'The fields are deserted, but I do not mind this in this too-full world, and I like the rain which drummed so hard this afternoon upon my umbrella that the internal combustion engines around me were inaudible. The longing for a world which is silent or only disturbed by "natural" sounds haunts one' (16 Oct 1940, L&F, ɪɪ, 185). How does one connect the silent world of fields and rain and friends who do not 'respond to culture' to the world of books and words, especially when one can see so clearly the ways in which privileging that natural world can be turned into an instrument of destruction?

Thus Forster's reading of Acton is one which pushes ironically towards the limits of its own assent. It is also a reading which is willing to challenge the notion of the stable text – indeed, will purposely destabilize, even deconstruct, that text to expose the degree to which it is susceptible to its own indictment. And yet at the same time, by that active engagement with the text, he recovers from it his own purpose as both reader and writer. It is, significantly, a purpose that is as ambivalent as the process by which its statement was arrived at. The 'nineteen century stuff' is something he must believe in, sometimes in his own despite, certainly with an awareness of the degree to which it belongs to a past that he does not have any illusions about recovering. Over and over again during this period he recurs to this idea: 'I don't believe that the present fabric of society is going to survive. . . . I don't feel *of* anywhere. I wish I did. It is not that I am déraciné. It is that the soil is being washed away' (letter to Hilton Young, 15 Feb 1940, L&F, II, 172). But he cannot simply hand on the Lord Acton in him without showing up its flaws and limitations.

However, so soon as *he* speaks, the utterance is transformed. Lord Acton's own words are different in *his* voice; what was certain and absolute and 'finely put' for Acton becomes unstable, edgy, capable of being turned upon its head and, most tellingly, put to the sterner political test of Forster's present moment. Throughout the thirties Forster was becoming increasingly aware of the difficulties of the authoritative, pontificating voice, even though it is during this period that he began broadcasting and then writing a column of commentary in *Time and Tide* and, later, in the *New Statesman and Nation*. But, if 1934 is the year in which he became the first president of the National Council for Civil Liberties, it is also the year in which he wrote to Isherwood concerning his public activities in connection with the Sedition Bill,

I think it is sensible and suitable, this alteration between fuss and calm. . . . It is the right conduct for our time – better than all calm, and far far better than all fuss. But if the war started, I don't know what would be right. The very meaning of words would change, and 'war' be the most meaningless of them all.   (9 Aug 1934, L&F, II, 123)

From such a perspective and within the even more agonizing context of 1940, Acton's words could hardly bear the more nearly univalent meaning they carried in 1900.

It is important to emphasize the phrase in the letter to Isherwood, 'the very meaning of words would change', when one turns to a consideration of the essays in the 'Second Darkness' section of *Two Cheers for Democracy* and, of course, the pamphlet essay 'What I Believe'. For the statements made in those essays do not constitute a compendium of extractable quotations. Their language is exploratory and probing, not fixed in Lord Acton's Indian rock. What must be emphasized is that Forster used language with a sense of its instability built into his own discourse. But that, unfortunately, is not how these essays have been read. They have rather been submitted to a reading that is essentially assaultive and often combative; that is, the text becomes a space that can be strip-mined and abandoned, each nugget that is uncovered tossed into the bin labelled 'Forster's Thought'. But where it came from, the chemistry of its composition and context are ignored. The statements remain inert matter and, to the degree that they can be used to construct a political programme that Reader A can subscribe to, both the statements and their author are pronounced acceptable. But, if Reader B sifts about in the bin and does not like what he finds, then both they and their author are scorned, called soft, irrelevant, dated or quaint, the worn-out fragments of a long-discredited liberal humanism (a response as likely to come from the Right as the Left). To read this way, however, is to read against the grain of Forster's writing. The last thing these often-quoted statements are is inert; the worst way to read them is as if they were detachable apothegms, an anthology of wisdom bits, or, as readily, of useless saws.

These statements draw their life from their place in the text; dug up they die. This is, of course, a version of the same problem I alluded to earlier with Montaigne's essays. For the reader's engagement with both Montaigne's and Forster's texts is very similar – it is to observe the thought as process rather than conclusion, to observe contradiction and irresolution not as symptoms of failure and confusion, but as evidence of that 'intellectual honesty' that constitutes the 'duty' Forster spoke of in the Acton entry. Certainly one can probably find in his writing more contradiction than Forster himself recognized and reveal him as captive of the very ideologies he thought to have unmasked. There is very likely no text that could not be submitted to such a procedure, especially with the full benefit of hindsight. But that hindsight was not Forster's in 1938 or 1941. As the war was shaping up, it was all too easy to fall in with an official line or at least to say nothing that would challenge it. His friend Hilton Young criticized him precisely for what Young called a lack of 'self control', a failure to 'stifle our complaints and control our individual choices, for a common good: (quoted in L&F, II, 174). Forster would have none of this:

> I feel that I am dissecting *not* humanity but the toils in which the human spirit and body have been caught. . . . The closing down of criticism, and the division of criticism into 'responsible' and 'illegitimate' are two of the things I am out against, and whose victory would in my judgment hasten the coming darkness.
>
> (17 Nov 1939, L&F, II, 169)

The letter from which this is taken was prompted by Young's response to the pieces Forster was writing for the *New Statesman and Nation*: 'I am so very sorry dear Hilton that my little things in The New Statesman have distressed you.' Two of them, reprinted in *Two Cheers* as 'Post-Munich' (10 June 1939) and 'They Hold their Tongues' (30 Sep 1939), are extraordinarily risky speculations on that coming darkness as at least partly due to the moral and intellectual abdication not only of those 'who have gagged their countrymen for their country's sake' (*TC*, p. 29), but also of those who recognized that evil and did not speak. But Forster takes no high moral line here. In darkness one cannot see, and Forster's vision is only more acute in so far as it recognizes its incapacity. The defining stance is never exhortatory, but rather interrogative; the world he is living in is barely comprehensible, an 'unexplored and equivocal state'. 'All is lost if the totalitarians destroy us', he asserts, but then the terrifying corollary, 'all is equally lost if we have nothing left to lose' (p. 22).

If the world is equivocal, so is the response. 'Post-Munich' is, of all Forster's essays, the most divided on itself, the most purely reflective of its occasion: 'The world won't work out, and the person who can realize this, and not just say it and lament it, has done as well as can be expected of him in the present year' (p. 24). The essay is such an act of realization; in both historical and linguistic terms, it eschews all certainties. It begins with the sense that the conviction of 1938 that war was imminent is now in 1939 attenuated and diluted. The terrifying has become familiar, a state of 'being half frightened and half thinking about something else at the same time' (p. 21). How, for example, to respond to news of the Chamberlain–Hitler agreement? There is immediate joy (especially in the House of Commons), but, just as immediate, the sense that something is wrong: 'Peace flapped from the posters, and not upon the wings of angels.' The observation allows the momentary recall of a larger consolation, but only by debasing it in the grotesque linking of the posters fallen in the gutter with the Christian icon of heavenly peace. The response of the essayist is to register this and then to return to the country and find 'satisfaction there in a chicken-run which I had helped build earlier in the week' (p. 22).

If it is impossible to read events, it is also impossible to assess the meaning of words – 'no slogan works'. It is in this context that an often-quoted and often misunderstood statement must be read: 'if Fascism wins we are done for, and . . . we must become Fascist to win' (p. 23). What that statement does *not* mean is, for example: 'In 1939 Forster had expressed the numbing conviction that to defeat fascism it would be necessary to become fascist.'[9] But it does suggest that fascism might nonetheless emerge if the fight against it involves the curtailment of civil liberties and an indifference to the individual in a privileging of state over person that both present legislation and national consensus seem to imply. It is interesting that this misreading, which occurs in the biography of Alan Turing by Andrew Hodges, is in its immediate context gratuitous – there is no reason for Hodges to bring in this allusion when he does – and, more significantly, it is part of a larger project of debunking or dismissing by trivializing the Forster who was supposed to have spoken so wisely in time of crisis. But Forster's wisdom consists in allowing no words and, particularly, not the words and slogans of 'our' side, to go unchallenged.[10] This is all the more necessary in a world where all statements (and the refusal, as well, to make statements) have become political acts.[11] Forster is certainly not advocating fascism, numbly or otherwise; he is not even implying that a way of defeating fascism is to become fascist (which really makes little sense). He is, however, registering the frightening paradox that, by not criticizing government, by not resisting the Sedition Bill or the Official Secrets Act, by acquiescing in the notion that the government can speak for the citizen, one is allowing fascism in, one is in fact doing the fascists' work for them.[12] So soon as the individual merges himself in some anonymous mass, he is giving up not only moral autonomy, but linguistic autonomy as well. When he is no longer in control of his language, fascism as a state of linguistic reification has arrived.

Thus the statement about fascism, as it resists simple closure and indeed turns into its opposite, shows how readily any statement that attempts to respond to the present can turn into a slogan. As he will do with the Lord Acton quotation a few months later, Forster turns words on their head. Such an act of linguistic play is implicitly deconstructive, as it both illustrates and undermines its assertion. As a statement that is its own illustration, it can hardly be considered prescriptive as if Forster were advocating a political position. The statement is, rather, trapped within itself, at one with what it identifies.

Because the essay neither claims any privileged insight nor can offer any solutions to the terrifying uncertainties of the present moment, it can only be certain of its own insufficiency as analysis. It proceeds from the double assumption that 'no slogan works' and 'the world won't work out' to the conclusion that 'the only satisfactory release is to be found in the direction of complexity' (p. 24). Although the essayist knows this, the essay itself never quite reaches that level of insight. There is an almost comic lameness in the attempt to find some way of coping – spending money (if one has it) on art, helping build a chicken-run in the country. The 'I' of this essay provides no counterweight to what it discloses. It knows no more than the 'unimportant and unpractical people' (p. 22) who can see but not act. The essayist as character collapses into his assumed audience. What results is a rhetorical impasse that reflects the situation that it set out to analyse. For, if to simplify is to accept slogans, not to simplify is to see through them and, paradoxically, to become paralysed by the realization that whatever one does involves 'betrayal of something good' (p. 23).

Implicit here is an attitude toward language that needs to be examined if Forster's accomplishment in these essays is to be understood. 'Our Deputation', published a few months before 'Post Munich', provides a useful text for that purpose, particularly as it illustrates one of the central insights of *A Passage to India* – that the line between language as meaning and language as noise is enormously difficult to draw even if one must never cease the attempt.[13] The essay describes a deputation from the Council for Civil Liberties to the Home Secretary, Sir Samuel Hoare, in December 1938 on the subject of the Official Secrets Act. In a scene that is presented as pantomime or puppet show rather than as discursive argument the deputation is imaged as some large creature (it 'straggled across Whitehall in the sleet, harried by taxis upon either flank. It jumped a bank of slush, slid upon the pavement . . .'), its destination 'the belly of a not very healthy monster'. The words that pass in the audience are appropriate to a master and a dog. When the Home Secretary enters 'all rose to their feet. The minister recoiled as if horror-struck by the commotion he had created. "Sit sit down, do please sit sit sit", he said. We obeyed.' As the scene progresses, language disintegrates, first into a pile of repeatable counters – 'very, very difficult difficult. . . . If you can can can help me . . . if you can can can can' (*TC*, p. 15) – then into a sequence of almost meaningless noises. There is a double disjunction, first between meaning and word, then between speaker and speech: 'They carry on like this: they begin a sentence deeply, gruffly, gently; it moves along like a large friendly animal; then it twitters, turns acid and thin and passes right overhead with a sort of whistling sound' (p. 16). The Home Secretary may empty words of meaning so soon as he utters them, but the Official Secrets Act which he is committed to upholding assumes that words not only have meaning but are dangerous. Similarly, those who fight (or form delegations) to speak what words they will, know how fragile words are, how capable of losing their meanings or being assigned falsely fixed meanings. There is always the danger of words becoming slogans, or so deformed as to be unrecognizable, or disintegrated into mere noise. However, if speech is risky, silence is even more so.

The piece that best illustrates this proposition and is, as well, the strangest and most moving of these 1939 essays, is entitled, appropriately enough, 'They Hold their Tongues'. It is a Dantesque parable that presents itself as a sketch for an as-yet-unwritten satire or, as Forster then goes on to suggest, the book for a ballet, on the subject of our present madness; it is set 'in the Ministry of Decontamination, in the Announcer's Parlour, and at the signs of the Walls Have Ears and the No Bird Sings'.[14]

The role Forster casts for himself here is a curious one. He is in part the satirist–parodist who keeps an appropriate distance as he confects an 'amusing entertainment' for some later 'intellectual day' when there can be laughter at a world where 'truth and falsehood . . . [have been] disintegrated into particles which are so small as to be equally useless'. But as the fantasy begins to take shape he realizes that it will not really be amusing, it 'will not be . . . genial'. Satire, in his view, is hardly amiable; his own attempt, for example, 'will have a touch of the rancid flatness which is a part of true satire – for Satire does not merely bite the victim, it lets down the reader too'. Rarely does Forster pitch irony into the more determined mode of satire; here he risks it, however, even risks sounding like Swift whom he cites in this context ('a few grim survivors, aristocrats, may appreciate it. Swift might contribute' *TC*, p. 28), although Swift is not a writer he read with much sympathy ('Swift's indignation . . . is too savage for me; I prefer Butler's in *Erewhon*' – 'A Book that Influenced Me', *TC*, p. 215). For the first half of this essay, the subtle and implicit discriminations of irony are put aside for the broader grotesqueries of a Swift or a Dante:

> There, beyond Phlegethon, he [Dante, but in fact Forster] would place them, and at the base of each tongue would nestle an atrophied brain. Their enormous ears are sewn against their scalps, so that they listen in with a vengeance. (pp. 28–9)

As in the *Commedia*, interpretation accompanies image:

> 'Here', says Virgil, 'is the recompense of those who have gagged their countrymen for their country's sake, instead of praising their God. Here are the chiefs of police and the card-indexers, and the takers of fingerprints, and Creon, King of Thebes, who issued the fatal edict, and the silencers of Lorca. Look at them, take warning from those dribbling gullets and, while speech is yours, speak.' (*TC*, p. 29)

However, it is not as a fantasist, but as the singer of Beatrice, as the poet of love, that Dante enables Forster to bring the text back from the satiric to the ironic mode. As Forster's Beatrice echoes Virgil, she quotes John: ' "Speak, speak," she cries, "for in the beginning was the Word" '; as the essayist returns to his own voice, as he attempts to heed his own parable and speak, he continues the quotation. Yet this text from John and the subsequent allusion to Matthew have a curiously deprived or emptied function here. They are invoked not only to emphasize the dismal fantasy, but to supply a response and a recourse. This they cannot do; Forster is no Bishop Jebb and his scriptural tags work neither in his text nor in his time: 'As if by the intervention of Satan, all the old religious and moral tags work out wrong.' For the light 'which lighteth every man that cometh into the world' has now been devalued to the light that must be put out lest 'the air-warden report . . . him for beckoning to death'. And Matthew's text, 'where two or three are gathered together', does not work either where such neighbourliness, like the candle in the darkness, also constitutes a civil danger (*TC*, p. 29).

It is not only the texts themselves that no longer seem to apply; the very gesture of quotation, of a verbal connection to a past, becomes an anachronistic, useless act. The pastiche paragraph that mingles scriptural allusions and current events defines a world for which there are no longer any fixed reference points. But at this point the essay voice registers an interesting shift in tone. Instead of lamenting the past, he simply acknowledges its loss. He knows that 'the old order, when Fate advanced slowly, and tragedies were manageable, . . . has vanished from the earth', and he is 'not so foolish as to suppose that fragments of it can be salvaged on some desert island' (p. 29). Memory and habit remain, however. And they, rather than faith, help to reinterpret the text from 1 Corinthians that is here recalled with much of its echo gone:

> Descending with Dante . . . we seek subterranean streams, we adjust in some spiritual region the balance which has been upset for ever here, we rejoin our friends, we punish our victorious foes, . . . we see face to face, and know even as we are known. This is sometimes called faith. The honester word for it is habit. It is no more than remembering a tune, it is carrying a rhythm in one's head after the instruments have stopped.   (p. 30)

Such an inherently quietist posture is presented problematically. For some, like the essay's speaker, it is unavoidable (he belongs too firmly to that vanished past), although it is not necessarily admirable and not even clearly useful. In rhetorical terms one hears this disjunction as well. Scriptural rhythms counterpoint a terse Senecan syntax, but the two styles are kept separate. Furthermore, although Paul's words are not immediately contradicted by the events of the present, as were Matthew's and John's, quoting them may well be an act of self-deception, as the essay seems to acknowledge in full irony at its close: 'We do expect . . . that those who . . . look back from their intellectual day upon us, the tongue-holders, will accord us not only pity, which we fully deserve, but disdain' (p. 30).

Of course, the essay as artifact carries its past with it. Virgil, Dante, Swift, Blake, scripture are all embedded in it, and, to the degree that the essay makes us rehear them, its most dismaying insight, that they belong to a silenced world, seems temporarily postponed. That last word, however, 'disdain', neatly upsets such an illusion, for here, in a gesture very unlike Dante's, Forster ranks himself with the Celestines who make way for the Bonifaces of his own time, and does not hesitate to include himself among those who 'hold their tongues'.

Three years before this essay, in 'Does Culture Matter?', Forster had also used Dante as a 'test case': 'We have, in this age of unrest, to ferry much old stuff across the river, and the old stuff is not merely books, pictures and music, but the power to enjoy and understand them' (*TC*, pp. 100–1). Using Virgil's image of the souls in Charon's boat as a figure for his own reading of Dante, he suggests that, if people are no longer reading Dante, 'it is a sign that they are throwing culture overboard, owing to the roughness of the water, and will reach the further bank sans Dante, sans Shakespeare and sans everything'. That sentence is an example of the same rhetorical procedure I described in the previous paragraph, for what the sentence says is contradicted by how it says it. Shakespeare may be tossed overboard, but he is being jettisoned by means of his own language and to that degree he is being kept aboard. However, unlike Eliot, for example, who, a decade or so earlier, had used his cultural fragments privately and talismanically as an insulation against the quotidian and the vulgar, Forster here attempts to reinvigorate and reintegrate the pieces of a shared past. Forseeing a future 'sans Dante . . . sans everything', where work and play are split, 'the work . . . mechanical and the play frivolous', he does not, Jaques-like, retreat into melancholy. He observes rather that 'if you drop tradition and culture you lose your chance of connecting work and play and creating a life which is all of a piece' (p. 101).

Such a conclusion could not have been further from Eliot's concerns in *The Waste Land*, but the belief that there can be no gap between the ethical and the aesthetic is for Forster basic to everything he wrote. It anchors the political centre of 'What I Believe', an essay that was explicitly to deal with the writer's 'philosophy' and which in its unfolding became a complex 'credo' for the 'life which is all of a piece'. It was a commissioned article for the New York *Nation* to inaugurate its 'Living Philosophies' series; it was immediately reprinted in the *London Mercury*, and then as a pamphlet by the Hogarth Press. As a result it has less of the occasional quality of many of the other political essays. Its reaction to events is not so immediate, and, whereas it, too, depends on unresolved paradox, it employs a linear rather than a circular, self-displacing discourse. It does provide, as Forster indicated in his preface to the 1951 reprinting in *Two Cheers*, the 'key to the book', but not in the sense of a check list of propositions that are repeated elsewhere with variations that can then be explicated by reference back to this 'credo'. Rather, it is a key to the book by being a key to the person, and, in so far as it makes the case for the individual, it does so by putting its own individuality, its own sense of self, in question.

To a degree this has always been recognized, but in, I think, a rather unfortunate manner, particularly in the years following the posthumous publication of *Maurice* and the stories collected in *The Life to Come*, and, of course, following P. N. Furbank's biography with its 'revelations' about Forster's loves and lovers. No mention could be made in essay or book review of Burgess or Blunt, for example, no discussion of MI5 could be conducted, without the writer trotting out the (in)famous line, 'if I had to choose between betraying my country and betraying my friend I hope I should have the guts to betray my country', as if Forster were somehow the progenitor of a generation of vipers. 'Well, we know what "friend" really means', has been the usually unspoken response – but not always unspoken, as in Cynthia Ozick's assertion, '*Maurice* instructs us explicitly in what he understood by "friend"; . . . . The statement about betrayal cannot be universalized, and Forster did not mean it to be. Declarations about bedmates do not commonly have general application.' And then the critic concludes with a statement clearly meant to have 'general application' itself: 'Does it devalue the large humanistic statement to know that its sources are narrowly personal? Yes.'[15] Ozick was by no means alone in 1971 in such revisionist and belittling appraisals. Two months earlier, George Steiner concluded a considerably more acute review of *Maurice* than hers with the remark, 'In the light of an intensely spiritualized yet nervous and partly embittered homosexuality, a number of Forster's most famous dicta – it is better to betray one's country than a friend [*not* incidentally what the dictum dictates], "only connect" – take on a more restricted, shriller ambience.'[16]

Although one may note in passing that the entire tradition of the Western love lyric, from Sappho to Catullus, to Sidney, Shakespeare and Donne, could be described as consisting of declarations about bedmates having general application, one should nonetheless insist that 'friend' here brings no such sexual undertone with it, as the Dante allusion to Brutus and Cassius makes clear. This does not mean that Forster was not speaking personally, but one may do so without direct reference to the self. The poet Louise Bogan, writing of the relation of her life to her poetry makes this aptly clear: 'The poet represses the outright narrative of his life. He absorbs it, along with life itself.'[17] There are, moreover, very few universals that have not been arrived at without a detour through the particular. Indeed, one may well ask why it is permissible that one's sense of Jewishness, for example (and hence a particular experience of the nature of anti-semitism), should allow one to generalize about the human quandary, but similar experience deriving from one's sexuality should be considered a limiting or disabling factor.

But Forster can be misunderstood by those who share that sexuality as well as by those who, like Ozick, think homosexuality unnatural (and then blithely announce that Forster thought so too). Hodges, for example, faults him for not engaging his homosexuality openly (by not publishing *Maurice*, for example), and assumes that those statements about loyalty, friendship, the state were so many words, easy enough to speak from the secure enclave of King's.[18] But not only was he not thus 'enclaved' in the thirties (he did not, with the exception of a three years' partial residence, return to King's until after the war, almost a half century after leaving it in the first place[19]); he was directly putting himself at risk by such declarations. By making so public a commitment to these liberal values, he was in a sense daring himself to live up to them, and from his perspective in 1938 it seemed more than possible that he would be called to account. Over and over again in his writing from this period (letters, journals, broadcasts, essays), he reiterates this concern. Furthermore, one must not forget the central phrase of that sentence, 'I hope I should have the guts', for his sense of human limitation, of the 'deadness' of the human make-up that he refers to in 'Ferney', arises directly from an acknowledgement of such possibilities within himself.

That phrase is, too, a perfect example of the 'duty' he mentions in the Acton entry of the *Commonplace Book*: 'to talk this late nineteen century stuff with a twenty century voice'. It would have been so easy to say 'courage' instead of 'guts', so consonant with the high-mindedness he was advocating, but 'courage' would have been something of an evasive word in that context in so far as it might have blurred the real consequences of his actions. This rhetorical interplay of the colloquial and conversational with the formal has, in fact, been long recognized as a hallmark of Forster's style; what I am suggesting here is that it is a quality less of style than of thought, indeed of being. Put to a twentieth-century test, he may well need 'guts' more than nineteenth-century 'courage'. And he does not claim he has them; he only 'hopes' he has.

The essay is sufficiently well known to require neither paraphrase nor summary, but it does require a rehearing, away from the noise of partisan skirmishes. Listened to in this way, the essay's 'I' is a less daunting (certainly less monolithic) figure. He reaches towards moral authority, but he does not ever claim to possess it. He certainly is not able to locate it in any external givens, even if he finds some fragments he would still hold on to (democracy, parliament, the intellectual heritage of Montaigne and Erasmus). However, unlike most credos ('Credo' was the title in the *London Mercury* printing), there is no institution larger than itself to which the essay bears reference. For perhaps the most subversive aspect of its argument is its insight that all institutions finally fail. Our 'tragedy' is not that there are no decent people, but that 'no device has been found by which these private decencies can be transmitted to public affairs' (*TC*, p. 71).

This was a particularly alarming conclusion to reach in 1938. The First World War had clearly not made the world safe for democracy. But, if all institutions are seen to have failed, if the two cheers the essay musters for democracy are more a valediction than a salute, then the constructing of a creed by one who is temperamentally a non-believer (even if something of a mystic) may seem a hopeless and a futile gesture, especially at a time when chaos seems moments away. Yet the speaker is far from hopeless (far less so here than in 'Post Munich', for example); his voice remains steady and, when he offers his nineteenth-century stuff, it is remarkable how fresh it still seems. For, if the credo is directly in the tradition of Victorian liberalism, it is also a challenge to that tradition, particularly to its smugness, its Christian capitalism, its public-school morality. From his vantage at the 'fag-end of Victorian liberalism', as Forster described his situation in the immediately post-war essay, 'The Challenge of our Time' (*TC*, p. 54), he could still recover something from it – in particular, the notion of the individual as the reference point of value. Although a beleaguered belief at a time when violence threatens and dictators 'incite . . . [their citizens] to mass-antics' (p. 72) and even democracies forget their ideals 'as soon as the drums beat and the bombers hum' (p. 73), it is for that reason the more tenaciously held on to. This seems to me to be the context in which one must place Forster's valuing of personal relationships, friendship, loyalty, Swinburne's beloved republic of love and Keats's holiness of the heart's affections.

The ethical problems that arise from such a stance are easy enough to identify; indeed Forster, anticipating such objections, provided them himself in the later essay 'The Challenge of our Time': 'When there is a collision of principles would you favour the individual at the expense of the community, as I would? Or would you prefer economic justice for all at the expense of personal freedom?' (p. 56). To those who argue that that is a false dichotomy, one can have both, he replies that he has no faith in 'the people', for they are an abstraction of those in power (that was clearly a lesson learned in the preceding war years), only a faith in the individual. It is an answer, however, that leaves the problem unresolved, particularly during the rebuilding of 1946. But rebuilding for the body, planning for the body's needs, can too readily slide into planning for the spirit. Democracies can overstep that line without even being aware of doing so; dictatorships do it all the time as a matter of principle and policy. Does one, therefore, not plan, not build satellite communities (because they destroy the village life of one's childhood memories), not provide the necessary housing? The answer, 'I cannot equate the problem' (p. 57), only restates it in a different guise.

It is precisely in this inability to 'equate' that the tradition of Victorian liberalism is put to the test and found wanting. But as readers we accomplish little by rushing in with our pencils to mark up these texts for inconsistencies. The inconsistencies are rather the linguistic evidence of that 'individual' they are celebrating, the individual who is always 'running off the totalitarian rails' (p. 73). Refusing to be prescriptive, even consistent, the essays offer inconsistency as principle; too many consistent systems have revealed their incapacity. This is not much to hold on to and the essayist acknowledges as much. Like Montaigne, however, Forster makes his own stubborn inability to 'equate' into an instrument of clarification by his refusal to take anything on faith, even his own absence of belief.

7

The Creator as Critic

I   A THEORY OF LITERATURE?

Taken all together, the literary essays, a few exceptions aside, do not linger in one's memory. The powerful ethical impulse that marks all Forster's writing, especially those wartime essays of soul-making, is present here too, but it was not easily shaped into an aesthetic instrument. Yet it was not only the difficulty of casting ethical issues in aesthetic terms that constrained his writing on literature. More significant was his founding his thinking about literary matters on a theory of creativity that inevitably locked him into a defensive and contradictory position. On the one hand there was his often-reiterated insistence on the utter separation of the creative and critical faculties; on the other, his own practice, which is best situated in the space between those two supposedly exclusive states. 'The critical state', he claimed in 'The Raison d'Etre of Criticism', a talk delivered at a music symposium at Harvard University in 1947, 'is grotesquely remote from the state responsible for the works it affects to expound'. Imaginative literature is made in a state akin to sleep; writing is like 'let[ting] down buckets into the subconscious', it is speech before thought. Criticism, by contrast, is purely an activity of the waking state: 'It does not conceive in sleep, or know what it has said after it has said it' (*TC*, p. 112).

The literary essays provide both example and counter-example of this assertion, itself a restatement of a point made as early as 'Inspiration' (1913) and 'Anonymity' (1925), and again reiterated in the 1931 lecture 'The Creator as Critic'. Many of them are in fact distinct – though never 'grotesquely remote' – from the works they are 'expounding' (that verb does not adequately describe Forster's critical practice; 'explore' is more to the point). Most of these are book reviews; they are always agreeable, often startling, and sometimes contain sentences that, lifted from their ephemeral context, possess a genuine afterlife. There are some literary essays, however, that as a whole and not simply in isolated flashes do in fact rise above their occasions and enter their texts so directly, imaginatively and re-creatively that the resultant essay which contains the trace of that encounter can claim an equivalent, although by no means an interchangeable, status. The essay on Skelton, for example, is not the same as Skelton's poetry, but it is as much 'literature', it is as genuinely 'created' as the poetry which prompted it. However, before looking at those essays that would support this claim, it will be useful to determine what Forster meant by such terms as 'literature' and the 'literary'. A definition that Forster formulated very early in his career will provide a helpful starting-point not only as it focuses his concerns as an essayist–critic but as it helps us negotiate the problematic creative–critical dichotomy that his criticism rests on.

The occasion was a talk given in 1913 to the BA and MA classes at Government College, Lahore. There, in response to his own question, 'why do people write books?', he developed an answer that amounts to a definition of literature: 'A book is really talk, glorified talk, and you must read it with the knowledge that the writer is talking to you.' Quoting from Shakespeare, Gibbon, George Eliot, he observed that 'though what they give us is transfigured talk, it is talk. . . . Listen to the voice of the writer speaking to you; that is the only guide. Listen to him as if he was . . . actually present in the room. . . . Literature is the speech of a man which goes on living after the man has died' (KCC).

Of course, there was Forster 'actually present', endowing the statement, as a result, with an authority he did not necessarily intend. In so far as his audience was listening to the writer speaking, it was willy-nilly enacting the role claimed for it by the speaker. What further complicates the writer–reader model here is the disparity in education and experience between speaker and listener, reflected too in the imperial relationship of the Englishman instructing the Indian. Forster works to subvert these givens as much as possible. His own voice eschews a spurious complexity; it is, rather, gently instructive, seeking out the audience's assent through its own experience. It is a voice that he developed lecturing at the Working Men's College. All statements are illustrated, subdivided, examined from various angles. The voice is non-intimidating chiefly because it pretends to no special expertise beyond that of the experienced reader and it offers that experience freely to its auditors as they are imagined entering into a joint enterprise with him. It is this insistence on transaction, a refusal to take advantage of the authority that his situation confers on him, that paradoxically confers authority on the claims Forster makes for the literary act. He is not, as some imply, a priest performing the rites of a literary mystery. His procedure here and elsewhere is, rather, to demystify and desacralize, to turn worshipper into celebrant, and to blur the line between the sacred and the profane, and thus, whether he intended to or not, between creation and criticism.

The basic assumption here, that the speaking voice is primary, will turn out to be, in the context of all the literary essays, far less simple than it sounded in the Lahore talk. That voice is certainly something Forster listened for in his own reading. He located his ambivalence towards T. S. Eliot, for example, in a 1929 essay first published as 'Mr Eliot's Difficulties', in terms of his sense that Eliot covered that voice, that Eliot's poetry was fundamentally 'inhospitable': 'Most writers sound, somewhere or other in their scale, a note of invitation. They ask the reader in . . . [but] Mr Eliot does not want us in' (*AH*, pp. 92–3).[1] Such a judgement is, to be sure, not purely literary. Although as 'poet' and 'novelist' they were not in direct competition, as cultural figures they were. Forster's following Eliot in the Clark Lectureship a year before this essay gives a public focus to what was in both literary and political terms an essentially ideological conflict, and a paradoxical one at that. For it was Eliot's cultural project with its implicit political conservatism that alienated the 'liberal–radical' Forster in direct proportion as Eliot's radical literary project seemed inaccessible to the 'conservative' Forster.[2]

Indeed, it may be useful to follow Forster's lead and, as he did with his *Commonplace Book* entry on Lord Acton, turn the conclusion he reached there on its head, by observing that on one level Forster's response to Eliot's poetry can be described as twentieth-century stuff in a nineteenth-century voice. That is, Forster implies a decorum of reading that suggests the nineteenth-century novel: the writer is a host, the reader a guest, the underlying metaphor one of hospitality and invitation. (In a 1924 essay on Jane Austen, the metaphor seems at one with the text: 'I greet her by the name of most kind hostess' – *AH*, p. 145.) However, its twentieth-century content can most clearly be seen if we translate it into contemporary critical language – the language of Barthes, for example. From such a point of view, the quality whose absence Forster regrets is, in fact, that which defines the 'modern' text: 'In modern texts, the voices are so treated that any reference is impossible: the discourse, or better, the language speaks: nothing more' (p. 41). What Forster is thus doing from this point of view is privileging the 'classic' text, in which, to continue the quotation from Barthes, 'the majority of utterances are assigned an origin . . . either a consciousness (of a character, of the author) or a culture'.[3]

Barthes's distinction may be of some use, I would suggest, for an examination of Forster's critical theory (or set of critical assumptions that may be called a theory in spite of themselves, for no theory was ever stated as such, and, if pushed to state it, Forster would have disclaimed its presence). In the case of Eliot, for example, Forster looks for origins even as he registers the silence of the originating voice. Identifying the central emotion of the poem as 'horror', he makes the silence a function of the poet's inability to state that emotion openly; an inability, he argues, that results in Eliot's use of a baffling and riddling language that builds obstacles to interpretation into its own discourse. By tracing the cause of the silence back to the writer, Forster turns that willed silence into voice, the poem becoming, from this perspective, 'a personal comment on the universe, as individual and as isolated as Shelley's *Prometheus*' (*AH*, p. 92). The reader–critic has thus recovered voice from absence, the multivalent or equivocal becoming a means to establish the univalent or univocal. Or, as Forster stated the matter in his 1931 lecture 'The Creator as Critic', 'there is such a thing as a final interpretation of *Hamlet*' (KCC). There he was arguing against Wilde's assumption, found in 'The Critic as Artist', 'that a work of art has no fixed meaning'. Here, in the Eliot essay, the attempt to fix meaning results in such statements as: ' "The Waste Land" is about . . . the fertilizing waters that arrived too late. It is a poem of horror' (*AH*, p. 91).

It is perhaps unfair to call this a 'final interpretation'; it may amount to no more than a search for entry into a text that is strewn with 'outworks and blind alleys' (the critical vocabulary itself coloured by the war that Forster understood as the occasion of that horror). For at the essay's conclusion he does not attempt to generalize the reading that he has offered, but he does verify it out of his own experience; indeed he appropriates it to his own voice. It is a reminiscence

of a bright August morning in 1914. I am lying in bed. The milkman below calls as usual with the milk, and through the clink of the handle I hear him say: 'We've gone in.' This, in its small way, is the kind of experience that must have beset Mr Eliot, and rooted itself in the soil of his mind. Most of us forget such an experience, or do not feel it acutely. Only here and there does it expand and contort into

> The circles of the stormy moon
> Slide westward toward the River Plate,
> Death and the Raven drift above
> And Sweeney guards the horned gate.
>
> (p. 93)

Forster's essay prompted a curious letter from Eliot in reply: 'You are right about the "horror"; and may be interested to know that the first quotation I chose for "The Waste Land", before I hit on the more suitable one from Trimalchio, was a sentence from the end of *Heart of Darkness*, which you may remember ending with Kurtz's words "the horror . . . the horror".' However, Eliot concluded, ' "The Waste Land" might have been just the same without the war' (10 Aug 1929, KCC), which may be described as partly taking back what he seems to have conceded, for Eliot reserved the possibility that the 'horror' may have a purely personal reference which is only accidentally confirmed by history. Such a response, from Forster's point of view, could only support his main argument that the poet 'does not want us in'. It is necessary, however, to underline the contradiction implicit in the essay. For the observation, '[the poem] is just a personal comment on the universe' (*AH*, p. 92), cannot be reconciled with the belief in final interpretation, unless Forster did not mean much more by such a phrase than 'establishing the co-ordinates' of an interpretation. But even here he is on shaky ground, for, if the poet tells him he is wrong in what he identifies as the poem's givens, he has nowhere to go. He is safest when he listens for voice, but with a modernist text that will also turn out to be a perilous enterprise.

Unable to hear the writer in the poem, Forster gave voice to the text himself, creating it both out of a prior Eliot text, 'Sweeney among the Nightingales', and out of his own experience, a morning in 1914. But that is far from the voice that he had asked his Lahore listeners in 1913 to attend to, the voice of the 'writer speaking to you'. Forster as reader (i.e. listener) has been forced by the text to become writer (i.e. speaker), illustrating, in Barthes's terms, the proposition that 'the goal of literary work (of literature as work) is to

make the reader no longer a consumer, but a producer of the text'.[4]
He has, however, been forced into this position in his own despite,
for he is by no means a proto-deconstructionist. The thrust of all his
criticism is towards the stable text, towards discovering a final, even
if elusive, interpretation. But that impulse exists in tension with
another one, the observation that forms the core of the argument of
'Anonymity: An Enquiry', written three years before the essay on
Eliot, that 'a poem points to nothing but itself' (*TC*, p. 81). Indeed,
just as his political writing is grounded on the basically conflicting
claims of the individual and the community, that problem he could
not 'equate' as he stated it in 'The Challenge of our Time', his literary
criticism is itself based on two givens – final interpretation; the
anonymous text pointing only to itself – that are finally
irreconcilable. This set of contradictions, however, strikes me as
considerably less productive than that which marks those deeply
perplexing yet essentially encouraging essays of moral reflection
and choice. For here it seems to constrain him, even to undermine,
or, at least unmoor, his judgements.

It is in his handling of the idea of 'anonymity' that the problem I
have been discussing can be most clearly seen. It is, to begin with,
quite different from what is currently meant by 'absence'. His
anonymous, that is unsigned, texts still proceed from originating
voices even if these have shed all traces of the daily personality who
answers letters, dines out, and, if he happens to be Coleridge,
smokes opium and joins the Dragoons. They are anonymous in the
sense that they privilege word over speaker, poem over poet, but,
nonetheless, they are not objects in the common domain, available
for dismantling, critical or otherwise. On the contrary, 'a poem is
absolute . . . it is eternal and indestructible' (p. 81). Poems, more
readily than novels, illustrate the proposition that 'all literature
tends towards a condition of anonymity' (novels are too close to the
newspaper, to a discourse of fact); yet all arrangements of words,
from the tramline sign 'Stop' on its metal disc to 'The Rime of the
Ancient Mariner', 'are all of one family. . . . If there is on earth a
house with many mansions, it is the house of words' (p. 80).

Although he places the literary and the non-literary along a
continuum rather than across a divide, Forster would still like to be
able to identify the quality that turns words into that other state,
inadequately called literature. But he fails to do so, comparing the
attempt to 'explain[ing] the secret of the universe' (p. 81). What he
can describe less mystically, however, is what happens to the

reader, making that transaction the defining quality of the literary. The reader, guided by his own imagination, enters into 'co-partnership' (p. 84) with the writer. This is not something he chooses to do; it happens because literature, in Forster's view, transforms the reader 'towards the condition' of the writer, and 'brings to birth in us also the creative impulse'. Literature is impersonal, and that quality of anonymity involves both writer and reader: 'the poet wrote the poem, no doubt, but he forgot himself while he wrote it, and we forget him while we read' (p. 83).

Thus reading is allied with the creative rather than the critical faculty (the stirring of the creative faculty 'in *us*' – emphasis added). For Forster considered himself not a critic but rather someone like Woolf's 'common reader', the writer's 'fellow worker and accomplice' (*CE*, II, 2). (Woolf, however, gave greater importance to the critical faculty as she allowed the reader to turn from friend to judge; she also cast her net more widely in her defining of the literary.) Both Woolf and Forster thought of the critic as a professional, and often a journeyman professional at that, whereas they saw themselves as amateurs (specially privileged to be sure), like those Woolf described in 'How Should One Read a Book?', 'people reading for the love of reading, slowly and *unprofessionally* [emphasis added] and judging with great sympathy and yet with great severity' (*CE*, II, 11). But, even more emphatically than Woolf, Forster would not allow critics into the circle of sympathetic readers: 'this sense of co-operation with a creator . . . is the one step over which criticism cannot help' (*TC*, pp. 113–14), he insisted in the Harvard lecture in 1947. His 1931 lecture 'The Creator as Critic', although it also uses these arguments, does so with a difference, for his concern there is with those writers who were both creators and critics – Coleridge, James, Arnold, Joyce, Tolstoy and Dryden (KCC). The premise that creation and criticism are utterly distinct is by no means fully sustained by many of the details in the lecture itself. Indeed, his observation that in Coleridge's notes on Shakespeare 'there are moments when he seems almost to connect us physically with the movements and the characters in the drama' seems to concede the creative faculty to the critical. And in Arnold's case it is the creative faculty that is seen to give authority to the critical prose. Furthermore, Forster's own dual status (even though he would have protested half of that identification) must itself have clouded the issue. Who was addressing the Cambridge English Faculty in 1931? The creator or the critic?

The Cambridge lecture is, on the whole, more interesting for its local remarks than for its theoretical framework, which is very nearly a repetition of the argument of 'Anonymity'. One of these remarks not only accounts for Forster's tendency to restate key ideas in essay after essay, but suggests as well how (or why) the creator-critic never totally abandons the one activity for the other:

> The mere fact of writing out a book and perhaps of getting it published has an effect upon an author's mind. He's much more tethered to his ideas after they have been embodied than before; the next time he takes up his pen, the same ideas, by a process of association, will tend to recur, not always appropriately. I think this is the reason why writers as they get on in life are apt to repeat themselves . . . they are mesmerised by the previous occasion.   (KCC)

Furthermore, given the definition of art that Forster offered in 'The Challenge of our Time' – and the rhetorical circumstances of its statement in that essay – it is not surprising that he had difficulty keeping these two notions in their separate compartments. He spoke there from the standpoint of the 'creative artist' called upon to answer the challenge, who offered a belief in art as a suitable response to the ethical impasse that he characterized in the statement which I have several times invoked – 'But I cannot equate the problem.' The writer in this view fits into nobody's plans, for his discipline must come from within:

> He may wish to practise art for art's sake. That phrase has been foolishly used and often raises a giggle. But it is a profound phrase. It indicates that art is a self-contained harmony. Art is valuable not because it is educational (though it may be), not because it is recreative (though it may be), not because everyone enjoys it (for everybody does not), not even because it has to do with beauty. It is valuable because it has to do with order, and creates little worlds of its own, possessing internal harmony, in the bosom of this disordered planet.   (*TC*, p. 57)

But this was 1946; Forster's writing for years had not been predominantly 'creative' in the sense that he would have us subscribe to. Yet he still spoke there as the 'creative artist', implicitly aligning his own writing with the creative function, and this was possible because those qualities of order and coherence that constitute 'art' are at once ethical and aesthetic. The artist is by definition engaged in a response to 'the challenge', but in terms that have little to do with the increasingly irrelevant creation – criticism dichotomy.

Why then did he insist on it? In part, I would suggest, to provide the underpinning for what one may call his theory of the non- or anti-theoretical. It certainly allowed him the privileges of the amateur in the halls of criticism and gave a kind of good faith to his refusal to be either high priest or schoolmaster (persons, and hence institutions, that he disliked, chiefly, I think, because they *planned* so thoroughly). But it is no less a theory for all that it is unsystematic and idiosyncratic, and leaves room for the unpredictable and the inconsistent. As S. P. Rosenbaum has so persuasively demonstrated in his study of *Aspects of the Novel* as 'an anti-critical work of criticism', eclecticism is both form and substance, methodology and conclusion; the entire series of lectures is dominated by a profound ambivalence toward formalist *and* non-formalist ideas.[5]

Forster's critical project is not, one must emphasize, what it has sometimes dismissively been called – literary appreciation. But, because of his ambivalence toward the critical activity, he drew back from committing himself to a unified critical procedure, preferring to arrive at his conclusions through a metaphoric language that was directly a function of the text he was exploring, but which had neither to be generalized nor to be categorized at the close. It was a procedure that sometimes failed, but often served him well, especially when it allowed him to locate a text's defining voice. In 'The Creator as Critic', Forster found a similar tendency in James – to develop criticism out of metaphor – but thought it might have caused James to 'lose in accuracy more than he gain[ed] in charm' (KCC). It was nonetheless a risk he took himself, and indeed he often did lose in accuracy what he gained in charm. But it did allow him to get exceptionally close to his text, to talk as if from within it, but not to pretend to any legislative function from without. His was thus a critical practice that put greater stress on process than on conclusion. The critic does not know some truth about the text before he begins, but he sets himself a course of discovery that amounts, in practice, to a theory of reading.

II SOME APPLICATIONS

Along with 'Anonymity' Forster ranked 'Dante' as 'genuine examples of something I haven't otherwise achieved'. He described what he meant by this 'something' in a 1929 entry in his *Commonplace Book*, 'a process, as of a living thing developing'. The 'living thing' he identified as 'thought', following Gerald Heard's distinction between 'thought' (an emotion) and 'logic'. But 'it isn't the same as thinking things out, which only demands acuteness and pertinacity. *It is a single organic advance*, not a series of isolated little attacks' (*CB*, p. 52; emphasis added).

This description of the activity of the critic–reader suggests both Forster's sense of organic connection to the texts he is presenting, and his sense of the organic connectedness of his own unfolding perceptions about those texts. It also depends on his sense of relationship to his audience – in both cases the students of the Working Men's College ('Dante' was given as a lecture on 21 November 1907, and 'Anonymity' on 28 February 1924), a relationship projected through a voice that is a curious mixture of the intimate and the courtly (i.e. formally courteous). Syntax and diction are so simple as almost to suggest condescension, but that never occurs; clarity and precision are, rather, techniques for making the text speak itself with only the merest intervention of the lecturer. It could never be said of Forster as he said of Eliot in a 1949 essay:

> there are . . . two Mr Eliots who write criticism. . . . They differ according to the audiences they address. Most of the book [*Notes Towards a Definition of Culture*] is addressed to sophisticated and highly educated people, and it is, on the whole, not satisfactory. At the end of it, three broadcasts are printed; these . . . [are] lucid, considerate and assured.   (*TC*, p. 253)

Assuming an identity of interests between himself and his audience (whether it was the students at the Working Men's College, the concert-goers at the Aldeburgh Festival, or the anonymous broadcast audience that he always attempted to personalize and individualize),[6] Forster developed a lecturing voice that survived intact in his written discourse. Even the alterations he made in the interest of the written version do not disturb the sense of the text's oral immediacy, its 'lucid' and 'considerate' voice.

When Forster pondered Heard's distinction between thought and logic in 1929, the only essay conspicuously missing from his list was 'My Wood'. From the retrospect of his entire career, however, quite a few others should be included – 'What I Believe', 'A Letter to Madan Blanchard', 'Ferney', some of the music essays and several of the literary essays, especially those on poets and poetry. Although his writing about fiction derived inevitably from his own practice as a novelist, Forster wrote about poetry completely as an outsider, and from the perspective of the historian, neither as a contemporary nor as the creator–critic. Because accounts of his critical stance have been generalized from *Aspects of the Novel* and depend for the most part on the categories and vocabulary he offered there, his achievement in discussing poetry – or, more precisely, a poet through his poetry – has gone largely unnoted. To be sure, there are certain fundamental concerns common to all his critical writing, but his procedure is quite different in these essays. It is to engage texts by characterizing how the mind that made them works – that is, by finding what it is in the text that 'talks', and then talking through that voice. It is a process whereby Forster became an archaeologist of voice, his lectures, thus, a voicing of another voice.

'Dante' is one of the earliest essays Forster wrote. However in voice and rhetorical procedure, it is closer to the essays of the thirties and forties than to those, such as 'Macolnia Shops' and 'Cnidus', written at nearly the same time. But, like those essays contemporary with it, 'Dante' is a work of the historical imagination. What marks the difference is the speaking voice; an implied interchange with an audience is established. This is a very different quality from that sense of reverie or soliloquy that marks those essays that did not begin as lectures. 'As we journey through life', the lecturer begins the 'Dante' essay, making the poem's central activity the reader's as well, and also connecting the existential situation of speaker and listener. Both together move through a space constructed like each of the canticles of the *Commedia* itself, a series of narrowing concentric circles that here carry speaker and listener back to poet, text and time.

The essay takes its impetus from a set of three ethical problems: 'How shall I behave to the people I know? How shall I behave to the people whom I don't know, . . . to the government, to society as a whole, to humanity? . . . How shall I behave to the unknowable?' These problems are not only used to organize Dante's *oeuvre* (the first as it refers to the *Vita Nuova*, the second to the *De Monarchia* and the third to the *Commedia*), but are also offered as issues 'inseparable from our humanity' (*AE*, p. 146). It is an approach that allows us to see the process by which aesthetic judgements are simultaneously ethical; a historical framework establishes the a-temporal, and the impersonal derives directly from the personal.

Forster's procedure is to connect Dante to ourselves by means of questions concerning the ethics of human actions and relationships, and then to analyse and judge Dante's literary production by its implicit answers to them. Thus the *Vita Nuova*, 'half a diary and half a novel', is an example of an essentially failed answer to the first, for that text is read as if it were saying: 'I regard them as a means to something else' (*AE*, p. 149). Just as the text is moralized by this approach, so is the writer, for the conclusion to his analysis of the *Vita Nuova* concerns a 'defect in [Dante's] noble character: He cannot be fair to the commonplace' (*AE*, p. 153). The other side of this response, however, is the answer to the second question: although Dante 'did not behave well to people who bored him, he would have laid down his life for humanity as a whole. He loved humanity as it was never loved again until the eighteenth century' (p. 154). To examine the practical consequences of this 'love', Forster takes a detour into the medieval notion of the relationship between soul and body, Church and state, in order to explain how Dante could have invested so much hope in a 'German princeling' (p. 158) and a Holy Roman Empire which was neither holy, nor Roman, nor an empire. It is the utopian impulse behind this belief that commends itself to Forster (and which he connects to the present need to believe in the Hague Conference or some similar scheme designed to deal with the conflicts among nations). Its expression in *De Monarchia* is called both beautiful and wise.

> It would be hard to find a more just discrimination between the forces that make men alike and the forces that make men different – between the centripetal power that may lead to monotony, and the centrifugal power that may lead to war. These powers are reconciled in the orbits of the stars; and Dante's first and last word to us is that we should imitate the celestial harmony. (*AE*, p. 162)

The stars, of course, provide a ready link to the *Commedia*, the text that is made to answer the third question, but Forster's account of the poem enlarges the issue until question and answer become one, 'until [Dante] actually sees the Love that lies behind the Universe and moves the stars – until he actually knows the Unknowable' (*AE*, p. 163). Forster is clearly not able to follow him there, but he does not scant the *Paradiso* for the more dramtic *Inferno* or the more cleanly and human *Purgatorio*; Dante's account is '"authoritative"'; it seems as if he really did know, as if he has really been outside time and space, and has come back to us with news'. Nonetheless Forster is uneasy with a vision whose 'standpoint is not in this world' (*AE*, p. 167). He knows that he should not be, for the 'Love' that Dante hymns is central to his own values, but the tones are strange: 'though his words are full of love and beauty, they gather a certain terror as they pass through the interspaces, and they fall with a certain strangeness upon our ears' (p. 168).

The essay clearly has a particular resonance for the short stories of this period, anticipating both 'Mr Andrews' (1911; 'the word "broad [church]" quavered strangely amid the interspaces' – *CT*, p. 226) and 'The Machine Stops' (1909), especially the latter's culminating action of a shattering leap toward the stars that move by love. But the echoes are heard not only in the stories, for Dante seems to have occupied an important spot in Forster's repertoire of intellectual and imaginative allusions. He frequently recurred to him in his *Commonplace Book* and in his essays. Indeed, among the writers and writings of the past that he often invoked – the Bible, Sophocles, Shakespeare, Keats, Blake, Wordsworth, Coleridge, Voltaire, Gibbon – only Shakespeare and the Bible appear more often and more variously.

The strategies for entering the poetic text vary. Dante, for example, is so enormous and omnipresent a cultural artifact and so intimately connected to his own speculations, especially on the subject of love, that Forster did not need to construct a special access. Although the underlying assumptions of Dante's writing remain remote both in concept and detail, once the surface had been explicated Forster could establish a timeless (although not completely a-historical) relevance. It was a different matter with Skelton. There the otherness of the text, its separateness from us in time and sensibility, the degree to which it is not assimilable either to our experience or our sense of language are the generating premises. Thus some personal link or entrance becomes necessary. Visiting the clergyman poet's church in Diss, he remembers Skelton's lines 'that when ye think all danger for to pass / Ware of the lizard lieth lurking in the grass', and is startled to discover a carving of a lizard on the buttress of that church. He then observes, 'its appearance, combined with the long grass in the churchyard, helped me to connect the present with the past, helped them to establish that common denominator without which neither has any validity' (*TC*, p. 138). That last may be debatable as a general proposition – that the past is only valid in so far as it finds some echo in the present – but it is certainly familiar to us in all of Forster's writing about the past, the larger category in which much of his best literary criticism belongs.

The lecture was given at the Aldeburgh Music Festival in 1950, at the sea edge of Skelton's East Anglia, a geographical connection that remains present through the talk, as if that might help in the search for links between present and past. Its dominant quality is sound, its aim to make Forster's audience *hear* Skelton's voice, for, as Forster explains at the essay's close, 'that past . . . is alway too dim, always too muffled, always too refined' (p. 149). Skelton could break that silence better than most, a noisy coarseness being a reiterated motif in the many poems from which Forster quotes (the text was 'simplified for the purpose of reading aloud' [p. 135], in a quasi-paraphrase adopted to Forster's own voice): 'Philip Sparrow', 'Ware the Hawk', a poem to Skelton's 'wife' (although he was a priest), one to 'Mistress Isabel Pennell', one called 'Merry Margaret', satires on Cardinal Wolsey and against the Scots, the loud and lewd 'Tunning of Elinor Rumming', and, to close, the even louder 'Against a Comely Coistroun'. Forster does not make the point about coarseness at all pejoratively; on the contrary, it is the chief source of the sense of sound he is conveying. Even when the preacher in the poet rises above the din he has created to announce, at the close of 'The Tunning', that his main aim has been to denounce 'dirty and loquacious women', Forster doubts and 'wonder[s]' (p. 147): 'I detect a coarse merry character enjoying itself under the guise of censoriousness'; and he cites as an apt description of the whole a line from one of Skelton's Latin poems in which the poet describes himself as 'sing[ing] the material of laughter in a harsh voice'. He also singles out passages that suggest a less purely comic vein, for Skelton could be 'tender and charming, occasionally . . . devout and very occasionally . . . wise' (p. 148). But it is the noise that is primary, that and 'the poet's fearless and abusive character', which he listens for in all the poems he quotes from and in all the details that he accumulates of the life and times of this clergyman poet laureate who was once tutor to Henry VIII and is now relegated to literature textbooks almost exactly midway between Chaucer and Shakespeare, but despite the chronology, infinitely more remote from us than either. With both Chaucer and Shakespeare 'we know where they stand, even when we cannot reach them' (p. 137). But not with Skelton. He stands across a divide and only sudden bursts of sound are audible.

A remarkable quality of these two essay-lectures is their almost effortless conveying of an entirely 'other' human identity through carefully nuanced readings of the texts and through an almost novelistic creation of character and scene, especially in the case of Skelton. Two years earlier in 1948, at the first Aldeburgh Festival, Forster's lecture 'George Crabbe and Peter Grimes' also derived its critical procedure from a novelist's reimagining of a prior text as recovered by reimagining its creator's mind. In that instance Forster was something less than a complete outsider. He had twice before written on Crabbe,[7] and the second piece, read by Britten while he was in the United States at the start of the war, not only had turned Britten to Crabbe's poem 'The Borough' as the source for his opera *Peter Grimes*, but was also largely responsible for causing Britten's return to England in 1942.

What most interested Forster in Crabbe was the degree to which he was so utterly bound to place, to the Aldeburgh he both detested and could not evade. It was a relationship to a specific place that Forster generalized to England: 'To think of Crabbe is to think of England', he had begun the article that turned Britten back to the same English landscape he shared with Crabbe by birth. What Forster attempted to explicate to his Aldeburgh audience was this dense nexus of originating circumstances. He was particularly interested in the repetitions in the creator's life of his creations' imagined lives, and in what can be described as the geographical determinism that shaped them both. It was a response to Crabbe's poem and to Britten's music that was closely tied to his own mythology of place, to Wiltshire and Hertfordshire, places that function as characters in his imagination, and, like Crabbe's Suffolk, are metonymies for England. Furthermore, to the degree that Crabbe's poem was itself founded on a 'true' story, however much its details were now lost and its outlines rendered mythic, he wanted to explore the relationship between historical fact and the creative imagination. Somewhere along the line, he suggests, there may have been a Tom Brown, the name offered as the original of Peter Grimes, but he is only important to the process in so far as the 'creative imagination' finds him out and 'accrete[s] round him until he is transformed'. Although given Forster's theory of creativity, there can be no accounting for this process of transformation, he nonetheless attempts in this lecture to situate himself as close to the generating materials as possible, inhabiting in this exercise a palimpsest of minds – those of Crabbe, Britten (and his librettist, Montagu Slater), and of course Peter Grimes and his nearly mythic prototype, Tom Brown.

In each of these lectures the focus is on the intermediate space where reader, writer and text intersect. It is Forster's characteristic space, where much of his own writing occurred and whose 'geography' most interested him in the writing of others. His subject as a critic was neither the historical entity, the writer, nor the entirely autotelic text. Indeed, his subject was largely his own construct, and it was with something of a novelist's licence that he animated this fiction, filtering it through his own personality and values, and – in the form of the lecture – giving it a temporary embodiment in his own voice. When he succeeded, as he clearly did in these lectures, the result takes its place with the best of his historical writing – the Voltaire essays, *Pharos and Pharillon*. But it was not a method that could be generalized, for it depended too much on the vagaries of circumstance and sympathy in the encounter. Applied to his contemporaries, especially to those who wrote fiction, its results were less consistent. Not only would both text and writer naturally resist the archaeologizing impulse, but the implicit ethical preoccupations that underlie Forster's historical writing – the implied question, how is this text useful in the conduct of one's life? – would not necessarily find responsive material. Joyce, for example, slipped out of Forster's net almost entirely. And James, to whom Forster recurred almost obsessively in his diaries and private writings, was never the primary subject of an essay even though he was a felt presence in the early novels. (There should be a study of the anxiety produced by that most agitating of influences; it might provide a better explanation than has yet been offered for why Forster ceased to write novels.) But the most significant example of an uneasy collision of two writers, their personalities and values and their aesthetic and ethical assumptions in full display, occurred between Forster and Woolf. How their writing spoke to and of each other, and how recent critics have heard (and misheard) this conversation, will provide the conclusion – and the coda – to this study.

III   E. M. FORSTER AND VIRGINIA WOOLF

In looking for a way to define Beerbohm's accomplishment in the essay form, Virginia Woolf observed that what he 'gave was, of course, himself[,] this presence which has haunted the essay fitfully from the time of Montaigne'. What Beerbohm brought to his writing was 'the spirit of personality', but 'so consciously and purely' that it is impossible to determine 'whether there is any relation between Max the essayist and Mr Beerbohm the man'. 'Never to be yourself and yet always – that is the problem.' Achieving that doubleness, that state of impersonal personality (what Keats meant by the 'poetical character') was not simply a matter of talking agreeably. There is always the danger, Woolf warned, 'of trivial personalities decomposing in the eternity of print' (*CE*, II, 46), and many a journalist/essayist, however charming, even learned and brilliant his talk may be, has not skirted that danger. But Beerbohm was an 'artist', that is the important difference, and his best essays have as a result 'that indescribable inequality, stir, and final expressiveness which belongs to life and life alone' (p. 47).

What Woolf describes as Beerbohm's accomplishment is precisely what I have been identifying as Forster's. But the passage is interesting for quite another reason – that is, for its implicit linking of 'art' and 'life', especially in view of Woolf's question in her review of *Aspects of the Novel* a short time afterwards: 'what is this "Life" that keeps on cropping up so mysteriously and so complacently in books about fiction?' (*CE*, II, 53). It is a rhetorically effective question as it allows her to conclude her attack on Forster's 'unaesthetic attitude' with something of a flourish, but it is also disingenuous. Fidelity to the 'full and truthful record of the life of a real person' (*CE*, II, 99) is what Woolf herself describes as the defining quality of fiction in her second 'reply' to *Aspects*, the series of articles published as 'The Phases of Fiction'.[8] 'It is the gift of the novel to bring us into close touch with life' – these are Woolf's words, not Forster's. To be sure, they are qualified by her insistence on 'style, arrangement, construction', by her sense that 'the most complete novelist must be the novelist who can balance the two powers so that one enhances the other' (p. 101). But Forster never denied this. He even allowed 'pattern' into his list of 'aspects' until it led him to James, whereupon he dropped it at once and turned to 'rhythm' instead, an aspect that Woolf only glancingly mentions in her review.

But how different is Forster's rhythm from Woolf's 'style,

arrangement, construction'? It 'stitch[es the] book together from the inside'; it is defined as 'repetition plus variation'; it is the ordering principle of the Fifth Symphony and in fiction it is best illustrated by the work of Proust. Forster's concluding example, *War and Peace*, is Woolf's also, one of the books she cites of fiction as art. For Forster it is an 'untidy book. Yet, as we read it, do not great chords begin to sound behind us?'[9] Such a statement seems to acknowledge the presence of Woolf's two powers, although it is clearly weighted toward the untidy, i.e. the lifelike. However, this view of the novel as an untidy form, neither created according to nor analysable in strictly formalist terms, constitutes an important part of Woolf's own feminist critique of the man-made palace of art:

> Fiction was, as fiction still is, the easiest thing for a woman to write. Nor is it difficult to find the reason. A novel is the least concentrated form of art. A novel can be taken up or put down more easily than a play or a poem. . . . And living as she did in the common sitting-room, surrounded by people, a woman was trained to use her mind in observation and upon the analysis of character.   (*CE*, II, 143)

This passage comes from a 1929 essay, 'Women and Fiction' (1929 was also the year of *A Room of One's Own*), but Woolf had herself, the year before Forster's Cambridge lectures, raised the issue of the competing claims of 'art' and 'life' in an essay-review, 'Life and the Novelist' (1926). There she described the ways in which 'Life' insists 'that she is the proper end of fiction', but such claims, Woolf argued, are in themselves insufficient, for if only the 'froth of the moment' is present, then 'the work passes as the year 1921 passes, as fox-trots pass' (*CE*, II, 135). The other quality must be there in equal measure: 'To survive, each sentence must have, at its heart, a little spark of fire, and this, whatever the risk, the novelist must pluck with his own hands from the blaze.' The figure that opens and closes the essay, indeed that defines the space of the essay, is described variously as the 'mysterious room' or the 'solitary room', where the writer's 'body is hardened and fashioned into permanence by processes which, if they elude the critic, hold for him so profound a fascination' (p. 136). This space for creation has multiple meanings for Woolf; one of them is clearly related to Forster's dream state figured in the image of the bucket that goes down below our daily lives and comes up with that mysterious substance called 'art'. As

Woolf describes it, 'processes of the strangest kind' are going on 'in that solitary room, whose door the critics are forever trying to unlock' (p. 131). Not only is her language similar to Forster's here, but she also shares his sense that the two states remain radically distinct, as well as his suspicion of the critical faculty.

Although what happens in both room and bucket is a constant of the creative process, Forster's view, as S. P. Rosenbaum has argued, is essentially a-historical (all novelists together in the British Museum's circular reading-room). At the same time his is often a more formalist approach than Woolf's ideologically necessitated commitment to ideas of history and development. For Woolf the creating space is no mere metaphor; for the woman writer the room must be achieved in fact, and with that achievement something *new* will happen:

> So if we may prophesy, women in time to come will write fewer novels, but better novels; and not novels only, but poetry and criticism and history. But in this to be sure, one is looking ahead to that golden, that perhaps fabulous, age when women will have what has so long been denied them – leisure, and money, and a room to themselves.   (*CE*, ɪɪ, 144)

Stating the issues in this fashion intentionally blurs Woolf's and Forster's positions in the art-life or formalist–anti-formalist controversy. For Forster was far more of a formalist than Woolf could acknowledge (in part because his formalism depended on music rather than on painting), and Woolf, especially in her polemical writing, was considerably less of one than Forster assumed, or, possibly, could see. However, precisely because their quarrel cannot be cast in terms of either/or, and because it has often been misrepresented, usually to Forster's disadvantage, it is useful to observe the degree to which they spoke out of a shared set of assumptions, even if at certain times each could be oddly out of touch with the other's achievement. These shared assumptions will provide a reference for an understanding of the ways in which they viewed each other's writing and of their sometimes contestatory public discussions on the novel, art and life.[10]

Although they each had reservations about the other's writing, Woolf's were both deeper and more publicly expressed. Forster, by contrast, was a generous supporter of Woolf from the very start, as his 1915 review of *The Voyage Out* makes clear. There he suggests his problem with her sense of 'character', a problem he will recur to in all his subsequent writing on her: 'her chief characters are not vivid . . . when she ceases to touch them they cease, they do not stroll out of their sentences' (*AE*, p. 249). At the same time, however, he acknowledged the startling nature of her accomplishment: 'She believes in adventure . . . and knows that it can only be undertaken alone' (p. 250); 'her comedy does not counteract her tragedy, and at the close enhances it' (p. 252). The reader is urged to forget his 'local questionings' and to 'lift his eyes to where there is neither marrying nor giving in marriage, to the mountains and forests and sea that circumscribe the characters, and to the final darkness that blots them out' (p. 249).

In 1915, Forster was the established novelist (although only three years Woolf's senior), whose support clearly helped her gain a public. But on a personal level, in letter and conversation, his support was even more important. For nearly her entire career, certainly until well into the thirties – that is, through all her writing save perhaps for *The Years*, *Three Guineas* and *Between the Acts* – he was the one reader–critic whose response, as entry after entry in her diary attests, she most valued. 'Morgan is the only one, either side, that matters', she wrote in her diary on 17 November 1931,[11] the day after copying into it his letter of praise for *The Waves*: 'It's difficult to express oneself about a work which one feels to be so very important, but I've the sort of excitement over it which comes from believing that one's encountered a classic' (L&F, II, 110).

Woolf clearly depended enormously on Forster for confirmation of her own achievement, particularly as his praise enabled her to understand the shape of her future writing:

> I was thinking of another book – about shopkeepers, & publicans, with low life scenes; & I ratified this sketch by Morgan's judgement. . . . I think I am about to embody, at last, the exact shapes my brain holds. What a long toil to reach this beginning – if *The Waves* is my first work in my own style![12]

This trust in his judgement sits curiously alongside both her public questioning of his 'unaesthetic' response to fiction and her own clearly ambivalent reading of his fiction. In her essay in which she 'did Morgan', 'The Novels of E. M. Forster', she scattered praise here and there, but, the observation of local felicities apart, her argument moved to what was a foregone conclusion from its premises, that Forster was a failed Ibsen. He should have stayed comic and not tried to solve the problems of the universe is the conclusion. She found too many 'contrary currents' in his novels, an observation based on the assumption that the 'essential gift to a novelist' is 'the power of combination – single vision' (*CE*, I, 345). Forster's didactic tendency, she argued, collides awkwardly with his 'exquisite prose style', his 'acute sense of comedy'. For a novelist who herself wrote out of a powerful didactic impulse, especially in her later work (and whose earlier fiction is increasingly being read in these terms), this is something of a strange conclusion to reach. It is perhaps more revealing of the writer than of her subject.

Forster had seen a draft of this article before its publication (as she had seen one of his 1925 essay). His response was to defend his method – his 'double vision' – while acknowledging that he may not have succeeded with it 'through simple lack of the co-ordinating powers that Ibsen had'. That Forster conceded Woolf's point so quickly suggests that he believed it; certainly a letter he wrote at the same time to T. E. Lawrence implies this: 'Don't bother about reconciling the statements in my books with my conduct at the tea table. See whether you can reconcile the statements with each other, and you will find that you cannot, alas that you cannot. And even Virginia Woolf has discovered this' (9 Aug 1927, L&F, II, 80).

But in that same letter he made another point. Referring to his story 'Dr Woolacott', and to *Maurice* (neither of which Lawrence had yet read), he wrote, 'these are items which you must have in your mind if you want to sum me up. Virginia Woolf, deprived of the items, has just made the attempt.' Forster's point here may help explain Woolf's ambivalence to the fiction she did 'sum up'. For the quality in his fiction with which Woolf had least sympathy, the recurring strain of fantasy, is precisely the quality that identifies Forster's homosexual imagination.[13] Thus not only did she not have access to the fiction that makes this explicit, especially 'Dr Woolacott'; she did not make the connection between literary mode and person (textuality and sexuality, one might say in 1987) in the fiction she was dealing with, her own similar investigations in *Orlando* notwithstanding.

There was, I think, a fundamental incomprehension on both their parts of the other's sexuality. Woolf's note in her diary 'the middle age of b——s is not to be contemplated without horror',[14] has its counterpart in Forster's note in his *Commonplace Book* that '*women have got out of hand*'. He describes there how he had earlier spoken 'with feeble enthusiasm of women's rights', but twenty years later (1930) he wonders at the results: 'this, I begin to see, is sex-war' (pp. 59–60). These were private musings, however, which certainly did not directly enter their literary discussions; neither writer may even have been aware of their influence. But such responses did, nonetheless, colour their judgements. Forster's declining to review *A Room of One's Own*, although he wrote her an encouraging letter about it and in the Rede Lecture called it 'one of the most brilliant of her books', is part of this. So, too, in the same lecture, is his dismissal of *Three Guineas* as 'cantankerous' (*TC*, p. 249).

It is fair to say that Woolf's feminism bothered Forster, even that it limited him as her reader. However, he never pretended it was not there, even if he was not able to see how deeply it was tied to those aspects of her imagination that he could identify and assess. It is one thing, however, to describe these limitations; it is another to make Forster responsible for a half-century of misreading, to say with Jane Marcus, for example, that 'E. M. Forster and his ilk [!] could . . . by avoiding her ideas, praise passages of description and create the lyrical formalist, minor mandarin, for generations of critics to analyze.'[15] Not only did Forster consider Woolf (and help establish her) as a major writer, but she *was* a lyrical formalist, although much else besides. Indeed, the burden of my argument has been that they were both 'lyrical formalists', but that neither quite knew how to describe this quality in the other, nor could understand its relationship to the other materials in their fiction, including what one might describe as 'life materials'. Hence Forster's faulting her characters; hence Woolf's faulting his prophetic voice.

One might add that, as important and deeply interesting a text as *Three Guineas* is, one should not so readily write out of the Woolf canon *Jacob's Room*, *To the Lighthouse*, *Mrs Dalloway* and *The Waves* in order to inscribe it there. Furthermore, that text's radical argument and form are still deeply connected to those 'patriarchal forms' that, it is suggested, Woolf set out to overthrow. Marcus argues that 'A Society', *A Room of One's Own*, *Three Guineas* and *Between the Acts* are generically revisionist as a function of their subversive stance and argument. But the generic mixing here and in *The Pargiters* that was to be transformed into *The Years* and *Three Guineas* is not discontinuous with a similar mixing found throughout Woolf's prose, where it is by no means always subversive: for instance, in 'A Letter to a Young Poet', 'Middlebrow', 'Walter Sickert', 'Mr Bennet and Mrs Brown', 'The Captain's Death Bed' and 'Mr Conrad, a

Conversation'. It is, moreover, related to what has been described as a Bloomsbury approach to genre that was itself a function of the intensely verbal world they lived in. They practised conversation as an art as well as writing it. Woolf not only talked about painting but she composed a dinner party, as one would a still-life, in order to talk about Walter Sickert's painting with him, and then imagined that conversation as an essay.

The mixing of genres is a characteristic that is conspicuous in Forster's writing – 'A Letter to Madan Blanchard' is the best example, but one could also include 'Mrs Grundy at the Parkers', 'Me, Them and You', 'Our Deputation', 'Our Graves in Gallipoli', 'It is Different for Me'. Furthermore, it was not exclusive to Bloomsbury. Without tracing its literary history back through the nineteenth century (the 'imaginary conversation' would be an example), one can note Beerbohm's 'The Relic', an essay–memoir on a short story that he never wrote which becomes both that story and its critique. In a similar fashion, Woolf's 'A Society' is a story that becomes an essay that uses conversation to parody an Apostle's paper.[16] That Woolf appropriated this method for more radical purposes than her male contemporaries had (or could recognize) is certainly true. But, if Forster is less subversive than she, he is still subversive, his distrust of institutions and social organizations and their norms equally deep seated and similarly connected to his sexuality. His anti-fascist writing, as I have argued, is as vexed and vexing as her angry polemic. It is a distorting revisionism indeed that can turn him into an emblem of the fascist–patriarch, the presumptive object of Woolf's rage and scorn.

I think this needs emphasizing now, for Forster has been too readily held responsible for an odd assortment of contradictory social ills. Such a response would seem to attribute to him a quite extraordinary power, although those who hold him to blame are not always willing to concede this to his literary accomplishment. It is, however, an ultimately belittling approach, for if Forster is held responsible he is at the same time rendered irrelevant. What I have been urging, on the contrary, is a reading that is at once less polemical and less ideological than is usually undertaken, and one that is as much aware of those points where Forster's and Woolf's texts touch as of where they diverge.[17] This, of course, does not mean that one should gloss over Forster's inability adequately to assess Woolf's feminism. When he raised the issue in the 1941 Rede Lecture, he got himself badly tangled up – in part grumbling, in part conceding, in part dismissing. What he was unable to see, especially in *Three Guineas*, were the underlying connections Woolf had made there among fascism, pacifism, and feminism,[18] and this despite the connections that he had himself made in 'Post-Munich', for example, between fascism and those institutions mobilized to resist it. But not wanting war, and possibly even feeling against one's better judgement that the Munich agreement was a reprieve, are not the same as pacifism, which was a step Forster could not take (nor Woolf, for that matter, who might have argued that way in 1938, but faced with the reality of war in the Battle of Britain in 1940 seems to have rejected it as well[19]).

Forster's difficulty with Woolf's feminism, however, was not simply a matter of a blind spot. The more fundamental difference is related in a curious way to their art–life quarrel, and indeed to the totality of their intellectual orientations. For Woolf's feminism was necessarily tilted toward the future, its outlook essentially optimistic. Or, to put the matter in terms closer to those used in this study, it turned away from the past, denying that there was to be found the source of all value. Social institutions must change just as literary forms will change; the novel is not outside history, but bound intimately to it. Forster's entire project, by contrast, was an act of recovery of the past. And in 1941, when he had glimpsed, as he expressed it in 'Ferney', the 'deadnesses and depths' of which 'human make-up' was capable (*TC*, p. 336), that seemed a particularly endangered enterprise.

IV   POSTSCRIPT

'She liked writing' – the sentence occurs at the start of the Rede Lecture on Woolf; a bit further on Forster expanded the point: 'She liked writing for fun. Her pen amused her, and in the midst of writing seriously this other delight would spurt through' (*TC*, p. 240). This observation is closely connected to another one: Virginia Woolf was

> alert sensuously. She had an enlightened greediness which gentlemen themselves might envy, and which few masculine writers have expressed. . . . Her senses were both exquisite and catholic and were always bringing her first-hand news of the outside world. Our debt to her is in part this: she reminds us of the

importance of sensation in an age which practices brutality and recommends ideals.   (pp. 246–7)

This is just the sort of critical perspective that Forster manages best – one that is located simultaneously within the writer, within the text, within the time. It depends primarily on his ear, on his ability to hear the text talk, the transaction that he recommended to his Lahore audience in 1913. Although he does not isolate language as a separable element for discussion or analysis, he is nonetheless extraordinarily alert to the words in the text. But the words are chiefly interesting as they identify an authorial consciousness and describe how that consciousness is connected to its historical moment. The last sentence in the passage quoted above, for example, implicitly makes Woolf a political writer – that is, her style makes a political statement, just as observing that fact makes commenting on Woolf into a political reading.

The quality that Forster was most alert to – although it was the one that gave him the greatest difficulty in so far as it was connected to the problem of characterization – is what he described as her poetry: 'She is a poet, who wants to write something as near to a novel as possible' (p. 246). This was not, however, a way of reading reserved for Woolf alone. The poetic was, in fact, precisely the quality that he heard best in all the writing he was most responsive to. Speaking to and about this quality allowed him an entry into fiction in the terms he used for writing about poetry. If one situates all his comments on this quality in the context of his debate with Woolf on life and art, one can detect there an implicit *defensio pro se*, a justification of that double vision that they both recognized as Forster's 'method' but with differing assessments of its success. Two broadcasts, one on Lawrence, the other on Hardy, demonstrate this clearly.

Forster described Lawrence in a 1930 broadcast as essentially a poet, whose *The Plumed Serpent*, Forster's favourite among his novels, contained 'poetry that broods and flashes, the power to convey to the reader the colour and the weight of objects'. When in that talk he spoke of the relationship between the poet and the preacher in Lawrence, he was clearly thinking of certain of Woolf's comments about his own writing, comments such as 'the neat surface [she was speaking of *The Longest Journey*] is always being thrown into disarray by an outburst of lyric poetry' (*CE*, I, 344). For Forster's Lawrence was a novelist who depended on the equipment of both poet and preacher. 'If he hadn't a message, his poetry wouldn't have developed. It was his philosophy that liberated his imagination. . . . If he didn't preach and prophesy he couldn't feel.' From such a perspective, the fact that Lawrence's 'plots aren't well made, the books aren't aesthetic wholes' is not significant, for 'there is a satisfied feeling at the close' (16 Apr 1930, typescript, KCC).

Again, in a 1942 broadcast on Hardy, Forster made very much the same sort of observation. Hardy

> was by temperament a poet, and not a novelist at all. He had taken up fiction partly because he had to earn a livelihood, partly because he misunderstood his powers. He couldn't manage a plot, he was clumsy at narrative, and his characters seldom come alive. But he had a poet's intensity of vision – both of great and little things.   (24 Feb 1942, typescript, KCC)

Reading fiction as if it were poetry may seem like the most formalist of critical acts. In Forster's practice, however, it served a non-formalist privileging of life's open-ended variousness, what he described in *Aspects* via a musical analogy as 'not completion. Not rounding off but opening out.'[20] At the same time it allowed him to identify the formal means for achieving this. In another broadcast, 'The Art of Fiction', he returned to this issue, arguing once more, as he had two decades earlier, against the notion of consistency of point of view:

> the power to expand and contract perception (of which the shifting point of view is a symptom) . . . is one of the great advantages of the novel form, and it has a parallel in our perception of life. We are stupider at some times than others . . . the intermittence lends in the long run variety and colour to the experiences we receive.   (24 Nov 1944, typescript, KCC)

Here an anti-formalist position is being made to serve a formalist end; that is, a specific technique, 'shifting point of view', becomes in verbal terms the equivalent of 'significant form' in aesthetic discourse.[21]

The epigrammatic sentence, 'the pen always finds life difficult to record; left to itself, it records the pen' (*AH*, p. 150), in its Escher-like doubling, states the matter in its most interesting form. It occurs in the second of his Jane Austen essays, where Forster pondered his perception of Austen's fatigue in the recently published fragment

Sanditon. Austen was there, he explained, 'completely in the grip of her previous novels (p. 149), the pen, left to itself, was recording the pen. But, when he pushed that statement further and began to observe where her pen was leading her at those intervals when it was not merely repeating itself, what he discovered was not so much a record of life as a formal prelude to a new kind of literary sensibility: 'Character-drawing, incident, and wit are on the decline, but topography comes to the front.' He discerned a 'romantic flavour', a 'new cadence in [her] prose' (p. 150). A change is emerging that is not yet named; it can only be located 'in her mind – that self-contained mind which had hitherto regarded the face of the earth as a site for shrubberies and strawberry beds'. But now 'the Lady of the Lake is creeping out . . . followed by her entire school' (pp. 151–2).

Perhaps one should put to rest these slippery counters – life, art. They arose out of a specific discourse that can be historically fixed in relation to the debate over the applicability of the language of art and aesthetics to literature, a debate complicated by the need to redefine those terms for the aesthetic discourse itself as a result of the enormous changes in technique and sensibility marked by Impressionism, Post-Impressionism, Cubism and the rise of abstraction. In the Woolf–Forster contention, these were approximate labels at best, never wholly accurate either where their beliefs and practices met or where they diverged.

Nor has it seemed very useful to hold on to that other pair of terms, 'creation' and 'criticism'. They may have served Forster polemically, but they do not describe his practice, for his accomplishment in essay and story was far more of a piece than that dichotomy would allow.[22] Certainly, his assessment of the relationship between these two activities in Woolf's work even more accurately characterizes his own: 'Amongst all this fiction, nourishing it and nourished by it, grow other works' (*TC*, p. 244). It is an observation inseparable from its language, just as the quality of organic and generative interconnectedness that it both points to and illustrates is the defining quality of all Forster's writing. One is reminded of the forests and copses around Abinger, of the trees in Hertfordshire, wych elms and other kingdoms, that so rooted themselves in Forster's imagination.

Both collections of essays end with trees. In *Two Cheers for Democracy* 'The Last of Abinger' arranges fragments from the *Commonplace Book* – entries on the Blind Oak Gate, the Old Crab

Tree, Fallen Elms. In *Abinger Harvest* 'The Abinger Pageant' provides the epilogue, and, in the Woodman's words, the epilogue, or, perhaps more accurately, the refrain, for this study too – 'I know that though the trees alter the wood remains' (p. 348).

Notes

Source abbreviations are explained in the List of Abbreviations on p. ix.

CHAPTER 1. INTRODUCTION

1. Johnson's definition comes from his *Dictionary of the English Language*; that of Barthes from *Roland Barthes par Roland Barthes* (Paris: Le Seuil, 1975) p. 124.
2. Montaigne, 'To the Reader' ('je suis moy-mesmes la matière de mon livre'), *Essais*, in *Oeuvres complètes*, ed. M. Rat (Paris: Gallimard, 1962) p. 9; Francis Bacon, from the 1610–12 manuscript dedication 'to the most high and Excellent Prince Henry', in *Francis Bacon, Selections*, ed. P. E. and E. F. Matheson (Oxford: Clarendon Press, 1922) p. 43.
3. Elizabeth Bowen's distinction between novel and story is useful here. In contrast to the 'rational behaviour and social portraiture' that is the domain of the novel, the short story 'allows for what is crazy about humanity: obstinacies, heroisms, "immortal longings"' – Preface to *Stories by Elizabeth Bowen* (New York: Vintage Books, 1959) p. x.
4. Barbara Hardy, 'An Approach through Narrative', in M. Spilka (ed.), *Towards a Poetics of Fiction* (Bloomington: University of Indiana Press, 1977) p. 31; Peter Brooks, *Reading for the Plot* (New York: Vintage Books, 1984) p. 3.
5. Milan Kundera, 'Afterword: A Talk with the Author by Philip Roth', in *The Book of Laughter and Forgetting* (Harmondsworth: Penguin, 1981) p. 232. See also 'An Introduction to a Variation', *New York Times Book Review*, 6 Jan 1985, for a discussion of his sense of affinity with Diderot and Sterne. (The essay was written as the introduction to Kundera's play *Jaques and his Master*, a variation on Diderot's *Jaques le Fataliste*.)
6. Gérard Genette, 'Frontiers of Narrative', in *Figures of Literary Discourse*, tr. A. Sheridan (New York: Columbia University Press, 1982) p. 127.
7. This is how Hayden White describes Genette's distinction. 'The Value of Narrativity in the Representation of Reality', in W. J. T. Mitchell (ed.), *On Narrative* (Chicago: University of Chicago Press, 1981) p. 3.
8. A. Preminger, F. J. Warnke, O. B. Hardison Jr *et al.* (eds), *Princeton Encyclopedia of Poetry and Poetics* (Princeton, NJ: Princeton University Press, 1974) p. 637.

CHAPTER 2. WRITING BETWEEN THE GENRES

1. *Aspects of the Novel*, Abinger Edition, ed. O. Stallybrass (London: Edward Arnold, 1974) p. 17.
2. The lecture is titled 'Creation and Criticism' in the surviving typescript, but see letter to Charles Mauron, 5 June 1930, L&F, II, 93.
3. Transcriptions are taken from the facsimile edition (London: Scolar Press, 1978), but citations are keyed to Philip Gardner's edition (Stanford, Calif.: Stanford University Press, 1985).
4. Virginia Woolf, *The Pargiters* (London: Hogarth Press, 1978) p. 33. She made the same distinction in 'The New Biography'.
5. Claude Summers, *E. M. Forster* (New York: Frederick Ungar, 1983) pp. 148–52.
6. Oscar Wilde, *Complete Shorter Fiction* (New York: Oxford University Press, 1980) p. 258; 'The House of Judgement' was originally published in 1894.
7. See Judith Scherer Herz, 'The Double Nature of Forster's Fiction', *English Literature in Transition*, 21 (1978) pp. 254–65; repr. in A. Wilde (ed.), *Critical Essays on E. M. Forster* (Boston, Mass.: G. K. Hall, 1985) pp. 84–94.

CHAPTER 3. THE STORIES I: MYTHIC FICTIONS

1. *The Longest Journey* (New York: Random House, 1962) p. 165.
2. Ibid., p. 189.
3. John Milton, 'The Reason of Church Government', in *John Milton: The Complete Poems and Major Prose*, ed. M. Hughes (Indianapolis: Bobbs-Merrill, 1957) p. 667.
4. The description evokes Pan, although the incident suggests Hermes in his role as God of travellers.
5. *Mythology and Humanism: The Correspondence of Thomas Mann and Karl Kerényi*, tr. A. Gelley (Ithaca, NY: Cornell University Press, 1975) pp. 9, 101.
6. Kerényi, 'The Primordial Child in Primordial Times', in Karl Kerényi and Carl Jung, *Essays on a Science of Mythology* (New York: Pantheon Books, 1949) p. 73.
7. Kerényi in Paul Radin, *The Trickster: A Study in American Indian Mythology* (New York: Philosophical Library, 1956) pp. 185, 189. See also W. Otto, *The Homeric Gods* (Boston, Mass.: Beacon Press, 1964) p. 117; and N. O. Brown, *Hermes the Thief* (Madison: University of Wisconsin Press, 1947).
8. Patricia Merivale, *Pan the Goat-God: His Myth in Modern Times* (Cambridge, Mass.: Harvard University Press, 1969) pp. 180–91.
9. 'Orion, a ghost, but the sight of him gives physical joy as if a man of the kind I care for was in heaven' (Diary, 11 Jan 1908, KCC). See discussion of 'The Machine Stops' in Chapter 4.
10. Letter of Mann to Kerényi, 1945, in *Mythology and Humanism*, p. 126.

11. A slightly different version was used as the headnote to *The Eternal Moment* (1928).

12. See Fur, I, illustration on back of dust jacket.

13. Henry James, 'The Great Good Place', *The Complete Tales of Henry James*, ed. Leon Edel, XI (Philadelphia: Lippincott, 1962–4) p. 25; originally published in *Scribner's Magazine*, Jan 1900, and repr. in *The Soft Side* (1900).

14. The typescript is at the Humanities Research Center at the University of Texas at Austin.

15. See T. B. Huber, *The Making of a Shropshire Lad: A Manuscript Variorum* (Seattle: University of Washington Press, 1966) p. 208.

16. The original title for the story, 'Dummy', makes the generic classification clearer. Letter to J. R. Ackerley, 28 May 1927, Humanities Research Center, University of Texas.

17. Robert K. Martin, 'Forster's Greek: From Optative to Present Indicative', *Kansas Quarterly*, 9 (1977) p. 72.

18. On 30 April 1924 Lawrence wrote, 'Comment? Oh, it's very difficult . . . in my first avid reading of it I ended it, & laughed & laughed' (quoted in L&F, II, 56).

19. Norman Page, *E. M. Forster's Posthumous Fiction* (Victoria, BC: University of Victoria Press, 1977) p. 39.

20. Frederick Crews, *The Perils of Humanism* (Princeton, NJ: Princeton University Press, 1962) p. 14.

21. *The Longest Journey*, p. 43. Forster used this passage from 'The Birds' in his biography, *Goldsworthy Lowes Dickinson*, as the setting for Dickinson's first awareness of a world of passion and imagination. See Abinger Edition, (London: Edward Arnold, 1973) p. 18.

22. Alan Wilde, 'Depths and Surfaces: Dimensions of Forsterian Irony', *English Literature in Transition*, 16 (1973) p. 267.

23. *A Passage to India*, Abinger Edition (London: Edward Arnold, 1978) p. 235.

24. *Alexandria: A History and a Guide* (New York: Doubleday, 1961) p. 71.

25. John Donne, 'The Extasie', lines 71–2; Elegie XIX, lines 33–4.

26. Forster wrote in the small, fawn-coloured notebook, 'The Letter-Book to Mohammed el Adl: who died at Mansourah shortly after the 8th of May, 1922', for several years. It was begun on 5 August 1922; the last entry is dated 27 December 1929 (KCC).

CHAPTER 4. THE STORIES II: NARRATIVE MODES

1. Claude Summers, *E. M. Forster* (New York: Frederick Ungar, 1983) p. 251.

2. From the concluding note to his reading of the opening chapter at the 1951 Aldeburgh Festival. Quoted by Elizabeth Heine in her Introduction to the Abinger Edition of *Arctic Summer* (*AS*, p. xi). Forster repeated this observation to P. N. Furbank and F. J. H. Haskell in the *Paris Review* interview (1955), which was reprinted in

Kay Dick (ed.), *Writers at Work* (Harmondsworth: Penguin, 1972) p. 8.

3. James Malek, 'Persona, Shadow, and Society: A Reading of Forster's "Other Boat" ', *Studies in Short Fiction*, 14 (1977) pp. 21–7.

4. Herman Melville, *Billy Budd, Sailor*, ed. H. Hayford and M. Sealts Jr (Chicago: University of Chicago Press, 1962) pp. 126–7.

5. Ibid., p. 131.

6. In a BBC discussion with Crozier and Britten, Forster remarked, 'When I think of the play, before I think of anything else, I think of Billy' (12 Nov 1960, typescript, KCC). In the first issue of the *Griffin* (1951; the magazine of 'The Reader's Subscription'), Forster described their problem in the opera to have 'been how to make Billy rather than Vere the hero'. Earlier Forster wrote to Plomer that the libretto had to 'rescue Vere from Melville' (letter cited in Fur, II, 284). Plomer had written the Introduction to the 1947 British edition of *Billy Budd*. See Robert K. Martin, 'Saving Captain Vere: *Billy Budd* from Melville's Novella to Britten's Opera', *Studies in Short Fiction*, 23 (1986) pp. 49–56.

7. *Billy Budd*, II.ii, rev. version, libretto (unpaged).

8. In a letter to Britten, Forster made this demurral explicit: 'Billy *is* our Saviour, yet he is Billy, not Christ or Orion' (20 Dec 1948, L&F, II, 235). His attitude toward Christ is most directly stated in his 1959 presidential address to the Cambridge Humanists: 'I now come to the only original part of my . . . address, namely my attitude toward the character of Christ as the Gospels present it. I am unsympathetic towards it' (KCC).

9. T. Todorov, *The Fantastic* (Ithaca, NY: Cornell University Press, 1975) p. 25.

10. H. G. Wells, Preface to *Seven Famous Novels by H. G. Wells* (New York: Alfred A. Knopf, 1934; New York: Avenel Books, 1978).

CHAPTER 5. THE HISTORICAL IMAGINATION

1. See Martin, 'The Paterian Mode in Forster's Fiction', in Judith Scherer Herz and Robert K. Martin (eds), *E. M. Forster: Centenary Revaluations* (London: Macmillan, 1982) pp. 99–112.

2. The title assigned in the KCC catalogue to a memoir lecture given at Aldeburgh (n.d.).

3. He uses the phrase in a letter to Florence Barger, 16 Oct 1916, L&F, I, 243.

4. He uses the phrase in one of his *Egyptian Mail* articles, 'A Musician in Egypt', 21 Oct 1917 (KCC).

5. 'Sunday Music', *Egyptian Mail*, 2 Sep 1917 (KCC).

6. Jane Lagoudis Pinchin, *Alexandria Still: Forster, Cavafy and Durrell* (Princeton, NJ: Princeton University Press, 1977) p. 126.

7. See Ch. 3, n. 26.

8. The phrase is referred to in Gerald Monsman, *Walter Pater* (Boston, Mass.: Twayne, 1977) pp. 30–1.

9.   *Alexandria: A History and a Guide* (New York: Doubleday, 1961) pp. 37–8.
10. Hayden White, 'Fictions of Factual Representation', in Angus Fletcher (ed.), *The Literature of Fact* (New York: Columbia University Press, 1976) p. 28. See also *Tropics of Discourse* (Baltimore: Johns Hopkins University Press, 1978) p. 125.
11. Trilling's formulation is useful here: 'Even E. M. Forster, who makes so much of privacy, acts out in public the role of the private man, becoming for us the very spirit of the private life.' 'George Orwell and the Politics of Truth', *The Opposing Self* (London: Secker and Warburg, 1955) p. 156.
12. See G. D. Klingopulos, 'E. M. Forster's Sense of History: And Cavafy', *Essays in Criticism* 8 (1958) pp. 156–65, which argues that the Hellenism of the earlier novels 'was a nostalgia for blessed simplicity', whereas the later writing 'implied a recognition of complexity'. Klingopulos sees Cavafy as the critical factor in the shift, but, to sustain the argument, he seriously underrates the earlier fiction.
13. In 1917 Forster wrote to Carpenter, 'You know my Days and Dreams are in their bloodless little way, on the lines of yours. I am gradually learning that I cannot work except where I love' (23 Apr 1917, KCC). Also see Robert K. Martin, 'Edward Carpenter and the Double Structure of *Maurice*', *Journal of Homosexuality*, 8 (1983) pp. 35–46, for a discussion of Carpenter's importance for Forster.
14. 'The moment a memory is registered by the intellect is its last moment' (letter to J. R. Ackerley, 26 Apr 1922, L&F, ii, 24).
15. See S. P. Rosenbaum, 'Bloomsbury Letters', *Centrum*, new ser., 1 (1981) pp. 113–19, for a discussion of this essay in terms of the mixing of 'fiction and non-fiction . . . in both the public and private letters of Bloomsbury'.
16. 12 Feb 1915, in *The Letters of D. H. Lawrence*, ed. G. Zytaruk and J. Boulton, ii (Cambridge: Cambridge University Press, 1981) p. 283.
17. Letter to Barbara Low, 11 Feb 1915, quoted in Fur, ii, 10.
18. *Egyptian Mail*, 21 Oct 1917 (KCC).
19. Wilfred Stone, *The Cave and the Mountain* (Stanford, Calif.: Stanford University Press, 1966) p. 284.
20. In a letter to Clive Bell, 22 Feb 1914, quoted in Michael Holroyd, *Lytton Strachey: A Critical Biography* (New York: Holt, Rinehart and Winston, 1968) p. 111.
21. The phrase comes from a 1936 entry (*CB*, p. 101).
22. *Lytton Strachey: Biographical Essays*, ed. James Strachey (London: Chatto and Windus, 1960) p. 107.
23. Lytton Strachey, 'Gibbon', *Portraits in Miniature* (New York: Harcourt Brace, 1931) p. 164.
24. Ibid., p. 159.
25. Ibid., p. 163.
26. Ibid., p. 159.
27. P. N. Furbank, 'Forster and Bloomsbury Prose' in G. K. Das and J.

Beer (eds), *E. M. Forster: A Human Exploration* (London: Macmillan, 1979) pp. 161–6.

28. *Edward Gibbon: Memoirs of my Life*, ed. G. Bonnard (London: Nelson, 1966) p. 103.

29. Leo Braudy, *Narrative Form in History and Fiction* (Princeton, NJ: Princeton University Press, 1970) p. 268.

30. See Braudy, who emphasizes Gibbon's 'relative and pluralistic vision', which he relates to Gibbon's growing narrative power (ibid., p. 246).

31. Forster uses this quotation from Gibbon's *Autobiography* as a headnote to his essay (*TC*, p. 157).

32. 'Fog over Ferney', *Listener*, 18 Dec 1958, p. 1030.

33. Ibid.

34. In a letter to Ackerley two weeks after the essay's publication in the *New Statesman and Nation* Forster wrote, 'I was so delighted with your praise of the Voltaire. Few people will see that it is on a better level than most of my stuff' (16 Nov 1940, Humanities Research Center, University of Texas).

35. See Linda Hutcheon, ' "Sublime Noise" for Three Friends: Music in the Critical Writings of E. M. Forster, Roger Fry and Charles Mauron', in Judith Scherer Herz and Robert K. Martin (eds), *E. M. Forster: Centenary Revaluations* (London: Macmillan, 1982) pp. 84–98. Mauron translated nearly all of Forster's writing; he was a scientist, aesthetician and critic. Three years after this essay Forster wrote to Isherwood, 'the friend I miss even more than you is Charles Mauron, for the reason that he is working out, in his blindness and the darkness of France, some connection between mysticism and aesthetics' (14 Dec 1943, L&F, II, 204).

36. Cited by O. Stallybrass in the annotated index to *Two Cheers for Democracy* (*TC*, p. 406).

37. Montaigne, *Oeuvres complètes*, ed. M. Rat (Paris: Gallimard, 1962) III.2, p. 794; *Essays*, tr. J. M. Cohen (Harmondsworth: Penguin, 1968) p. 249.

38. Montaigne, *Oeuvres complètes*, III.12, p. 1028; *Essays*, p. 329.

CHAPTER 6. FROM PRIVATE SELF TO PUBLIC TEXT

1. The entries that were used in the Clark Lectures have been published as Appendix A in the Abinger Edition of *Aspects of the Novel*, ed. O. Stallybrass (London: Edward Arnold, 1974).

2. As here, references to Montaigne in this chapter appear in the text and take the following pattern: (1) volume, chapter and page in Montaigne, *Oeuvres complètes*, ed. M. Rat (Paris: Gallimard, 1962); (2) page in Montaigne, *Essays*, tr. J. M. Cohen (Harmondsworth: Penguin, 1968).

3. Montaigne as 'the subject and the object of the textual presentation' is the grounding assertion of Richard L. Regosin, *The Matter of my Book:*

Montaigne's Essais as the Book of the Self (Berkeley: University of California Press, 1977). See also Terrence Cave, 'Problems of Reading in the Essays', in I. D. McFarlane and Ian MacLean (eds), *Montaigne: Essays in Memory of Richard Sayce* (Oxford: Clarendon Press, 1982) pp. 133–66: 'The "linking thread" is . . . produced by the shadow of a writer reading and rereading his text in search of a "linking thread"' (p. 158).

4.   Forster's essay about the *Commonplace Book*, 'Bishop Jebb's Book', was first published in 1940 and reprinted in *TC*, pp. 181–4.

5.   See John O'Neill, *Essaying Montaigne: A Study of the Renaissance Institution of Writing and Reading* (London: Routledge and Kegan Paul, 1982).

6.   See ibid., ch. 5 ('Writing and Embodiment'); also Jean Starobinski, 'The Body's Moment', *Montaigne: Essays in Reading*, Yale French Studies, no. 64 (New Haven, Conn.: Yale University Press, 1983) pp. 273–305.

7.   Both essays were first published in the *New Leader*, 'Me, Them and You' on 22 Jan 1926, 'My Wood' on 15 Oct 1926. However, in *Abinger Harvest* the dates are given as 1925 and 1926 respectively. Forster's dating in *Abinger Harvest* is sometimes unreliable. 'Mrs Hannah More', for example, was first published in 1925, but is dated 1928; 'Salute to the Orient' appeared in 1921, but is dated 1923.

8.   'For us was Thy back so bent, for us were Thy straight limbs and fingers so deformed: Thou wert our Conscript, on whom the lot fell, and fighting our battles wert so marred. For in Thee too lay a god-created Form, but it was not to be unfolded; encrusted must it stand with the thick adhesions and defacements of Labour: and Thy body, like Thy soul, was not to know freedom.' Thomas Carlyle, *Sartor Resartus*, ed. C. F. Harrold (Indianapolis: Bobbs-Merrill, 1937) III.iv, pp. 227–8.

9.   Andrew Hodges, *Alan Turing: The Enigma of Intelligence* (London: Allen and Unwin, 1983) p. 254. It is worth reminding ourselves how difficult and dangerous it is to judge a moral response retrospectively. Forster's essay was written not only after Munich but a few months after the German invasion of Czechoslovakia, an event which Britain could probably have prevented. From Forster's perspective in June 1939, however, it must have seemed far less a turning-point than it now appears to have been: 'When Germany or Italy destroys an extra country we are upset for a shorter period each time' (*TC*, p. 24).

10.   For Hodges, Forster's silence about his homosexuality, his not publishing *Maurice* and the later stories, his reticence about his personal life are the givens that undermine his supposed moral authority.

11.   Forster's letter to Edmund Blunden, who had argued against Oxford's decision not to send a delegation to Göttingen's bicentenary celebrations makes this point emphatically: 'You fear that Oxford's abstention may be political. I expect it is and don't see how it could help being, and her acceptance would have been political also.

Germany has chosen to make every relationship political, and no non-political relationship with her appears to be possible' (1 May 1937, L&F, ii, 150).

12. In a letter to C. Day-Lewis, Forster provides another version of the same statement: 'Either we yield to the Nazis and they subdue us. *Or* we stand up to them, come to resemble them in the process, and are subdued to them that way' (30 Oct 1938, L&F, ii, 161–2).

13. See, in particular, ch. 10; p. 126 in the Abinger Edition (London: Edward Arnold, 1978).

14. This strain of fantasy persists in Forster's writing, although many of the pieces were unpublished. 'What Does it Matter: A Morality' was posthumously published in the *Life to Come* volume, and 'Little Imber' and 'From a Forthcoming Blue Book' (the latter a very amusing satire on broadcasting described by Forster in a marginal note on the manuscript as 'nice nonsense') were published in the *Arctic Summer* volume.

15. Cynthia Ozick, 'Forster as Homosexual', *Commentary*, 52 (1971) p. 85.

16. George Steiner, 'Under the Greenwood Tree', *New Yorker*, 9 Oct 1971, p. 169.

17. Louise Bogan, 'From the Journals of a Poet', *New Yorker*, 30 Jan 1978, p. 62.

18. In *With Downcast Gays: Aspects of Homosexual Self-Oppression* (London: Pomegranate Press, 1974) Hodges writes, p. 18, 'Since the choice was unlikely ever to be presented, this was an easy, if startling, claim to make. The real choice for Forster lay between damaging his reputation and betraying his fellow homosexuals. Alas, it was his reputation that he guarded and gay people whom he betrayed.' Hodges somewhat moderated this antagonistic stance in the Turing book, but Forster is, of course, a much more peripheral figure there.

19. Forster was in temporary residence (six weeks each year) between 1927 and 1930, when he accepted a fellowship following the Clark Lectures.

CHAPTER 7. THE CREATOR AS CRITIC

1. The date given in *Abinger Harvest* is 1928. It was, however, written for the *New York Herald Tribune*, 12 May 1929.

2. Both F. R. Leavis and W. Stone provide useful discussions of the cultural politics of the period, particularly in terms of the either/or critical response to Joyce and Lawrence. A letter Forster wrote to the *Nation and Athenaeum* after Lawrence's death aligned him with the Lawrence 'side' ('he was the greatest imaginative novelist of our generation') and provoked a flurry of letters in response, T. S. Eliot's among them. See Fur, ii, 164; F. R. Leavis, *D. H. Lawrence, Novelist* (London: Chatto and Windus, 1955) p. 10; W. Stone, *The Cave and the Mountain* (Stanford, Calif.: Stanford University Press, 1966) p. 382. Also see C. E. Baron, 'Forster on Lawrence', in G. K. Das and J. Beer

(eds), *E. M. Forster: A Human Exploration* (London: Macmillan, 1979) pp. 186–95.

3. Roland Barthes, *S/Z*, tr. Richard Miller (New York: Hill and Wang, 1974) p. 41.

4. Ibid., p. 4.

5. S. P. Rosenbaum, '*Aspects of the Novel* and Literary History', in Judith Scherer Herz and Robert K. Martin (eds), *E. M. Forster: Centenary Revaluations* (London: Macmillan, 1982) pp. 55–83.

6. A 1942 broadcast conveys this with an extraordinary clarity and poignance: 'I don't know what you're like, you, my unknown listener. As I write this script down in the country – and the country is charming now: the trees, the sunlight and the clouds have never seemed more indifferent to the conduct of man – or as I walk to deliver it through the battered London streets which have a war-time strangeness not wholly depressing – : or as I sit perched in the studio pretending to improvise it whereas it is actually all written out – : I keep speculating where you are sitting and standing, what you are like': 'My Debt to India', in BBC series *Some Books*, 19 Aug 1942 (typescript, KCC).

7. The first time was in 1932, when he wrote the Introduction to *The Life of George Crabbe by his Son* (1834), in the World's Classics series (London: Oxford University Press, 1932). The second was in a broadcast, 'George Crabbe: The Poet and the Man', printed in the *Listener*, 25 (1941) pp. 769–70. Britten described reading it in his 1951 Introduction to the opera: 'During the summer of 1941, while working in California, I came across a copy of *The Listener* containing an article about George Crabbe by E. M. Forster. I did not know any of the poems of Crabbe at that time, but reading about him gave me such a feeling of nostalgia for Suffolk, where I had always lived, that I searched for a copy of his works, and made a beginning with "The Borough". . . . It is easy to see how [Forster's] account of this "entirely English poet" evoked a longing for the realities of that grim and exciting seacoast around Aldeburgh'. In Philip Brett (ed.), *Benjamin Britten: Peter Grimes*, Cambridge Opera Handbooks (Cambridge: Cambridge University Press, 1983) p. 148.

8. See Rosenbaum in Herz and Martin, *Forster: Centenary Revaluations*, p. 77. 'The Phases of Fiction' was originally intended to follow E. Muir's *The Structure of the Novel* in the Hogarth Press series 'Lectures on Literature'.

9. *Aspects of the Novel*, Abinger Edition, ed. O. Stallybrass (London: Edward Arnold, 1974) p. 116.

10. A recent attempt to assess their relationship is less than even-handed. David Dowling, in *Bloomsbury Aesthetics and the Novels of Forster and Woolf* (London: Macmillan, 1985) p. 92, suggests that Forster thought 'Woolf's novels . . . nothing more artistic in themselves than mass-produced "little" cups'. (Dowling is referring here in a quite misleading way to the concluding image of the Rede Lecture, where Forster spoke of 'her career as a triumphant one . . . she brought in the spoils. And sometimes it is as a row of little silver

cups that I see her work gleaming. "These trophies", the inscription runs, "were won by the mind from matter, its enemy and its friend" ' – *TC*, p. 252.) Dowling argues that Forster 'never admitted Woolf's artistry' until *To the Lighthouse* (*Bloomsbury Aesthetics*, p. 91), that 'for Forster it is life or people first, and art second' (p. 224), and that his own writings were 'at their best . . . parables whose shape almost approximates a work of art' (p. 225). Dowling's observation that Forster 'concentrat[ed] always on the reader rather than on the thing read' has a certain truth to it, especially if one applies it to Forster's critical writings, but it does not lead to the conclusion that Dowling draws, that 'it is paradoxical that [Forster] . . . should write such unartistic books' (p. 226). The most useful part of the study is the least polemical, particularly its discussions of Fry, Bell and Mauron as they define 'Bloomsbury aesthetics'.

11. *The Diary of Virginia Woolf*, iv: *1931–5*, ed. Anne Olivier Bell (London: Hogarth Press, 1982) 16 Nov 1931, p. 54.
12. Ibid., p. 53.
13. In her diary for 6 July 1920, referring to 'The Story of the Siren', Woolf wrote, 'Morgan might boom, though I don't, as a critic, see altogether what the reason is' *The Diary of Virginia Woolf*, ii: *1920–4*, ed. Anne Olivier Bell (London: Hogarth Press, 1978) p. 52. In her summing up a few years later she referred to Forster as 'an uneasy truant in fairyland', and the world of *The Celestial Omnibus* as a 'freakish land where boys leap into the arms of Pan and girls become trees' (*CE*, i, 348).
14. 12 Mar 1922, in *The Diary of Virginia Woolf*, ii, 171.
15. Jane Marcus, 'Liberty, Sorority, Misogyny', in C. Heilbrun and M. Higgonet (eds), *The Representation of Women in Fiction*, Selected Papers from the English Institute, new ser., no. 7 (Baltimore: Johns Hopkins University Press, 1981) p. 64.
16. See ibid., p. 85; also Edward Hungerford, 'Is "A Society" a Short Story?', *Virginia Woolf Miscellany*, 1983, pp. 3–4.
17. Several of their essays make suggestive pairings: Woolf's 'Thunder at Wembley' and Forster's 'The Birth of an Empire', or Woolf's 'Memories of a Working Women's Guild' and Forster's 'Me, Them and You' and 'The Challenge of Our Time'. Forster's essayistic persona seems less preformed in all of these, his role less clearly that of 'the writer'. The chief difference in the pair of Wembley essays, for example, is that *he* is *there*. Both subject and object exist prior to being a source of metaphor or generalization. This is less true of the second pair. Woolf is as much the essay's subject as are the letters the essay is introducing. The double time focus of the Woolf essay – the 1913 meeting, the 1931 memory – complicates the essay self in ways that have no analogue in Forster's essays.
18. See Victoria Middleton, '*Three Guineas*: Subversion and Survival in the Professions', *Twentieth Century Literature* 28 (1982) pp. 405–17; also Naomi Black, 'Virginia Woolf and the Women's Movement', in Jane Marcus (ed.), *Virginia Woolf: A Feminist Slant* (Lincoln, Nebr.: University of Nebraska Press, 1983) p. 191: 'Virginia Woolf's

feminism was political because it responded to notions about power and social structure, and because it reflected a specific organization and programmatic history.'

19.   Given the date of Woolf's death (1941), Marcus's comment on this point is curious: 'She did relent in her pacifism enough *towards the end of the Second World War* to advocate defense from the enemy' (in Heilbrun and Higgonet, *The Representation of Women in Fiction*, p. 71; emphasis added).

20.   *Aspects of the Novel*, p. 116.

21.   In the interest of that much too sharply drawn art–life controversy this point is often missed. Dowling's conclusion, for example, that except in *A Passage to India* Forster's 'narrative voice mocks the very aesthetic shape he is erecting' (*Bloomsbury Aesthetics*, p. 232), is a function of his 'Lubbock' bias and prevents his understanding of the technical (and, in his terms, artistic) possibilities of 'shifting point of view'. In fact, Forster's use of this term corresponds closely to Fry's reading of A. C. Bradley: 'the creation of structures which have for us the feeling of reality' (quoted ibid., p. 18).

22.   In 1935, when Forster was putting *Abinger Harvest* together, he wrote to Isherwood, 'there is plenty of stuff and much of it quite good in patches, but slight terrors steal over me. It's been so ineffective, when one considers the course of affairs, and it's so imperfect when compared with real writing' (16 Jan 1935, L&F, II, 129).

Index